The front cover depicts the Company house flag, with the painting by Alexander Harwood (1873-1943) of CITY OF LONDON (1871) super-imposed on it. The back cover is a reproduction of the front page of a Company brochure issued in 1928.

South Pier, Aberdeen in stormy weather, and where many ships came to grief in such conditions over the years.

(Aberdeen Library)

THE ABERDEEN STEAM NAVIGATION COMPANY LTD

Graeme Somner

Published by The World Ship Society
Gravesend, Kent DA12 5UB
2000

FOREWORD

The history of the Company is mainly based on the Minute Books covering the period 1836 to 1925, now held at the University of Aberdeen, and those from 1940 until 1974, at present held at the National Maritime Museum, Greenwich, supplemented by information extracted from Lloyd's Register of Shipping, Lloyd's List and Board of Trade records as well as numerous other publications.

Unfortunately, the whereabouts of the Minute Books for the period 1926 until 1939 is unknown, which leaves a slight gap in my knowledge of the happenings of that period.

Like all minute books the world over, the contents vary on the whims of the writer and this is very much so as far as The Aberdeen Steam Navigation Company is concerned. One has to take into account the long period they cover and the number of individuals that must have been involved in writing them up. Some of the writers went to great lengths to chronicle quite mundane items such as the appointment of a steward, whilst another missed out an important incident involving the loss of a ship ! One is therefore left quite often to "read between the lines" and I trust that I have done that correctly. Whilst the condition of the books themselves are good, the same cannot always be said of the writing - at some periods it was very difficult to decipher and I can only hope that I managed to transfer the facts accurately.

I hope you enjoy reading the story as much as I enjoyed delving into the records. I never did have the opportunity to sail on any of the vessels and unfortunately now, never will.

Graeme Somner
Christchurch, Dorset
January 2000

ISBN 0 905617 92 4

CONTENTS

FROM THE HIGHLANDS TO ST PAUL'S

The Aberdeen Steam Navigation Company can be traced back to 1821, when a group of citizens of Aberdeen came together and commenced trading under the name of the Aberdeen & London New Shipping Company (the word *New* was dropped after a few years), offering sailings from Aberdeen, in the Highlands of Scotland, to the heart of London, within sight of St Paul's Cathedral. The men behind these sailings were merchants, shipowners and shipbuilders of the City of Aberdeen, the most prominent amongst them being George Thompson (shipowner), John Lumsden (merchant), and Robert Catto (merchant), who owned the smack NIMROD. Other individuals in the group were George Forbes (merchant), George Elsmie, junior (iron founder), Peter Mathieson (shipbuilder), Robert Duthie (shipbuilder), and James Brebner (merchant). The first vessel to sail under this new company's banner was NIMROD. She was joined by MANSFIELD, which after being rebuilt at Aberdeen, was registered in the ownership of George Forbes and John Lumsden. It would appear that all subsequent ships were registered as owned by different groups of names, and it is not clear who actually managed the Company, except that the names of John Lumsden, Robert Catto, and George Elsmie, junior, occur most frequently.

It was not until 1824 that a third ship was introduced on to the sailings. This was another Dorset-built (the first two ships had also been constructed at Lyme Regis) vessel appropriately named BON ACCORD (the name forms part of the crest of the City of Aberdeen conveying goodwill). These three were joined in 1826 and 1827 by a further three new vessels, BETSY, DUKE OF GORDON and TRUE BLUE, but this time all built at various Aberdeen yards.

In 1827 John Duffus & Company (trading as the Aberdeen & London Steam Navigation Company), introduced steam on to the London sailings. John Duffus & Company had been shipbuilders for many years, with a yard at Footdee, and this venture into shipowning was supported by many of the shareholders in the Aberdeen & London Shipping Company John Duffus & Company constructed the wooden paddle steamer QUEEN OF SCOTLAND for this service - their first steamer. The local newspaper *The Aberdeen Journal* in its edition of 18th April 1827 says :

"On Thursday last, we had the gratification of being present at the launch of the first steam vessel which has been built at this port. If we may judge by the admiration which this magnificent ship has existed, among naval and scientific persons, as well as those acquainted with steam navigation, we may safely pronounce her the finest of her class not only for a frame of timber which cannot be surpassed, but which has been put together in a manner that would do credit to any of the King's Dockyards. Her length is that of a 36-gun frigate - she has a spar deck and poop, with two splendid cabins, separate from the sleeping

QUEEN OF SCOTLAND from a painting commissioned in 1843.

(Kingston upon Hull Museum)

compartments, which are ranged along the side of the ship, and all entering from the main deck. These berths have removing stanchions, which, if necessary, would enable her to carry 15 guns on a side. She will be propelled by two engines of 75 horse-power each, and is calculated to carry, beside her machinery, fuel etc, three hundred tons. Not withstanding the unfavourable state of the weather from the incessant rain, a vast concourse of spectators had assembled at an early hour, and seemed delighted with the beautiful airs played by the Band of the Aberdeenshire Militia. At a quarter past one o'clock, the QUEEN OF SCOTLAND majestically glided into her future element, amidst the cheers of the multitude, the Band playing "God Save the King". This superb vessel has been built by Messrs J. Duffus & Co and her engines constructed at their extensive establishment here; and if the QUEEN OF SCOTLAND is to be considered a fair specimen their work, it will bear a comparison with that of any of her class in the kingdom. The launch was conduced by Mr Ronald, the master builder, in a style which did him credit; and we were much pleased to observe the accommodation afforded by the proprietors of the neighbouring dock-yards, whose servants appeared to vie with each other in rendering every assistance in their power on this novel occasion. We sincerely wish Messrs Duffus & Co every success in the prosecution of this now most important branch of nautical science."

Subsequently an article appeared in the newspaper during May regarding the trials of QUEEN OF SCOTLAND :

"On Saturday last, the beautiful steam ship QUEEN OF SCOTLAND lately launched here, went out of the harbour on trial, in the presence of a great concourse of spectators, who were crowded on the pier to witness the gratifying sight. When she started from her moorings, it was the first time her paddle wheels had gone round; and although her engines did not appear to us to be at half their speed, she went out in magnificent style. Contrary to the opinion of many people, who had predicted she would roll heavily, she appeared to do quite the reverse, and to swim as easily in the water as a duck; and we understand, there never was a finer or more comfortable sea boat. The engineers and work people had been much fatigued in getting her ready, and as frequently happens "the more haste the less speed"; about 120 mechanics etc accompanied her to sea, and as it blew fresh, it was impossible to land them. About midnight as we are informed, the "Queen's" cooking apparatus was put in requisition, and her hungry subjects contrived to set her Majesty on fire, but whether from over roasting or over boiling, we have not been able to learn; but we are happy to say, that very little damage was done; it might have been worse; the fire was put out in good earnest; and the "Queen" stood off to sea with her canvas only, and was descried in the morning at a great offing, turning to the windward in grand style against a flood tide. A signal having been made from the pier, on Sunday, the steam was set *on, and she returned to the harbour at 3 o'clock p.m. For days past, crowds have been visiting this fine vessel, and examining her splendid cabins and accommodations. We observe that she will remain in the harbour for some time, and we recommend those people who have not seen her, to judge for themselves."*

Originally advertised on 14th May to sail on 17th May, but because the vessel was still not complete, a later advertisement on 7th August (see below), changed the sailing to the 22nd.

THE STEAM PACKET FOR LONDON
QUEEN OF SCOTLAND
Alex. Lovie, R.N., Commander.
This Splendid, New, and Powerful STEAM
PACKET SHIP will sail from :
ABERDEEN, Wednesday, 22nd inst
LONDON, do , 29th inst.
ABERDEEN, do , 5th September.
Cabin passengers - - - - - £5
Steerage do - - - - - £2-10/-
including Provisions and Steward's Attendance.

Merchandise and Rough Goods, Freight as per Sailing Vessels.
Carriages, Horses and Light Goods, Freight as per Steamers
'twist London and Edinburgh.

The Proprietors assure the Public every exertion has been used
to provide comfortable accommodations, and Male and Female
Stewards, capable of performing the duties of their situations.

Arrangements have also been made with Messrs Smith and Sons,
Galley Quay, London (the second above Tower Stairs) for
Landing and Shipping Goods, without any additional charges to
Shippers.

Apply to JOHN LUMSDEN & CO, Castle Street
or JOHN DUFFUS & CO, Footdee.
Aberdeen, August 7, 1827.

However, despite the fact that she was formally registered on 17th August 1827, other technical problems had been identified by then, so she could not be handed over, and it was not until January 1828 that *The Aberdeen Journal* reported:

"The beautiful steam ship QUEEN OF SCOTLAND, Captain Walker, made her first voyage when she sailed from hence on the afternoon of Saturday 22nd December 1827, arrived at London on Tuesday thereafter. From the thickness of the weather she was obliged to come to anchor 16 to 18 hours during her voyage, but completed the run notwithstanding the late period of the season, in the same time as is generally required in summer by the finest of the steamers between Edinburgh and London."

It was reported that on her first voyage she carried as well as passengers, 210 head of cattle and 700 boxes of salmon. She was joined on the sailings in 1829 by DUKE OF WELLINGTON also built at Aberdeen. In 1835 a third paddle steamer joined this fleet, CITY OF ABERDEEN built by John Scott & Sons of Greenock. Launched on 3rd February 1835, she was handed over by the builders on 5th June which made three steamers available for service.

AMALGAMATION OF SAIL AND STEAM

By November 1835 rivalry on the Aberdeen to London sailings was fierce with steam competing with sail for the trade. The Aberdeen & London Shipping Company were operating five sailing vessels, whilst the Aberdeen & London Steam Navigation Company (managed by John Duffus & Company) had three steamers in service. As in many cases, the shareholders in the ships had shares in both companies, it seemed beneficial that the ships operated as a group. An amalgamation was agreed, with the new company taking the name of the Aberdeen Steam Navigation Company, the principal partners behind the new company being James Brebner, George Elsmie, junior, and Robert Catto. John Duffus & Company was to initially undertake the maintenance of all the vessels, both steam and sail. The objectives of the new company were to concentrate on the London to Aberdeen sailings, carrying passengers, general merchandise and livestock (principally cattle), and to introduce sailings from Aberdeen to Hull. At no time were the sailings combined.

The amalgamated companies' first sailing was undertaken by the steamer QUEEN OF SCOTLAND in October 1836, with the sailing vessel NIMROD taking the next sailing. None of the sailing vessels originally owned by the London & Aberdeen Shipping Company (except BON ACCORD and DUKE OF GORDON) were formally taken over by the new company and within months of the amalgamation the sailing vessels MANSFIELD, NIMROD and TRUE LOVE were sold to other owners for service elsewhere. DUKE OF GORDON was sold soon afterwards in March 1837 which left BON ACCORD the only sailing vessel in the fleet. During the summer season of 1837 and 1838 a call at Sunderland was introduced.

In December 1837 discussions began with the Aberdeen & Hull Shipping Company (principal shareholders being James Forbes and William Elsmie) regarding the possibility of taking over the goodwill of their trade, but in September 1838 the offer made was rejected. However, the pressure on the Company of having to run a steamer to Hull every week instead of every 10 days to compete with the competition, made the Company consider a revised offer for the goodwill of the Hull trade. This was finally accepted in July 1839, and gave the Company a monopoly of trade between Aberdeen and Hull. With this acquisition came three vessels, the smacks SUPERIOR (1814), THETIS (1826) and FLORENCE (1831). THETIS only remained with the Company for a short time before being sold in February 1840.

Changes in the fleet took place in April 1838 when the wooden paddle steamer DUCHESS OF SUTHERLAND (1836) was purchased for £13,500 from the Moray Firth & London Steam Packet Company of Inverness. In July 1840 the last original sailing vessel, BON ACCORD (1824), was sold. The fleet was now made up of four steamers and three sailing vessels, with the vessels trading from Aberdeen to London and Hull. The Company withdrew DUKE OF WELLINGTON from the Hull sailings in 1843 as the trade was no longer profitable, and then maintained the Hull service with sailing vessels only.

At the end of December 1843 the insured value of CITY OF ABERDEEN (1) was £17,000, DUCHESS OF SUTHERLAND £15,000 and DUKE OF WELLINGTON £6,750. No record of insurance is mentioned for the sailing vessels so presumably the Company covered the risk itself. The Minute Book of this period records that boiler problems on all the steamers were the cause for delays to the sailings, and this was to remain a problem for some years to come, despite continual replacement.

The first new sailing vessel built for the Company was the schooner PARAGON in 1842. She was joined in the fleet during 1844 by a further three schooners, ABERDONIAN (1840), LONDON (1840) and WILLIAM HOGARTH (1841), when the Company bought for £3,600 their competitors on the London sailings, Nicol & Munro of Aberdeen. This then gave the Company a monopoly on the route. WILLIAM HOGARTH, however, only remained in the fleet for a short time before being sold in 1846.

IRON REPLACES WOOD

In 1841 John Duffus & Company, trading as the North of Scotland Steam Navigation Company, approached the Company to ask whether they would buy their steamer NORTH STAR (which had recently run ashore) and the goodwill of their London to Inverness trade (calling also at Lossiemouth and Burghead) - John Duffus & Company also owned the small paddle steamer SATELLITE (196/38) but there appears to be no mention of taking her over as well. She was, however, sold in February 1843 to owners in Calcutta. There was already fierce competition on the Aberdeen to Inverness route from the Leith & Clyde Shipping Company's VELOCITY (215/21), but at that time the Company deemed that trading conditions were not right to expand into that trade. Because of this competition, NORTH STAR had been frequently been chartered and was often to be seen in European ports such as Amsterdam. In July 1845 she was chartered to the Peninsular & Oriental Steam Navigation Company (in the name of Hartley Wilcox, Carleton & Anderson, as apparently under their Charter, P & O were at that time denied the right to run non-mail services in the Mediterranean) to operate three sailings from London to Leghorn and Genoa. She was found to be too small for the traffic on offer and completed her last voyage at London on 4th December 1845. Meantime, in October 1845, the Company purchased a majority holding in the North of Scotland Steam Packet

Company with the purchase of 3,000 shares at a cost of £33,000, and so now controlled the operation of NORTH STAR from that time. By December 1845 the sailing vessels LONDON and WILLIAM HOGARTH had joined NORTH STAR on the Inverness sailings.

One of the three steamers, QUEEN OF SCOTLAND was sold in January 1843 to Hull owners for the sum of £4,500, the figure being low because the vessel needed extensive repairs and also new boilers. Her place was taken in the following year by the newly-built CITY OF LONDON (1) from the Clyde shipbuilders, Robert Napier & Company for £32,000. She was the first iron-hulled vessel in the fleet. Various improvements were also made to other vessels during the early 1840s. At the end of 1844 the Company owned five steamers valued at £83,259, six sailing vessels valued at £6,350 as well as wharfage buildings, barges and lighters (on the River Thames) valued at £9,145. During the year of 1844 CITY OF LONDON (1) had made 27 voyages to London, CITY OF ABERDEEN (1) 26, DUCHESS OF SUTHERLAND 16 and DUKE OF WELLINGTON 20. The total mileage steamed during this time was 91,750 miles, the cost of which averaged out at 8/5d (45p) per mile.

At the time of the formation of the Company, the capital stock was 6,400 shares but, with the need to provide additional capital, this number was increased in 1839 to 6,740, in 1843 to 7,000 and in 1845 the capital stock was increased to £150,000 in 25,000 shares valued at £6 each. Profits remained constant with the sum being £38,994 in 1845, general cargo providing some 28% (£20,876) of the revenue, passengers 17% (£12,639) and livestock nearly 25% (£18,078) of the revenue. The greatest expenditure was on coal to the sum of £9,600 (28%), wages at £7,479 (21%), insurance and harbour dues at £7,782 (22%), with repairs to ships' engines costing £4,022 (12%).

In 1846/47 three new vessels joined the fleet. In May 1846 the Company took delivery of the sailing schooner named GAZELLE (as it was to turn out, also their last), which had been built at a local yard. In March 1846 an order was placed with Robert Napier & Company, Glasgow for two iron paddle steamers and a deposit of £15,000 was paid in July 1846. DUKE OF SUTHERLAND and EARL OF ABERDEEN were completed in March and July 1847 respectively, and the wooden paddle steamer DUCHESS OF SUTHERLAND (1836) was traded-in as part payment for these new vessels.

At the beginning of 1847 the book value of the fleet was as under:

CITY OF LONDON (1)(1844)	Iron paddle	£32,700
CITY OF ABERDEEN (1)(1835)	Wooden paddle	£21,000
DUCHESS OF SUTHERLAND (1836)	Wooden paddle	£10,760
DUKE OF WELLINGTON (1829)	Wooden paddle	£ 8,000
PARAGON (1842)	Schooner	£ 2,000
GAZELLE (1846)	Schooner	£ 2,561

13

CITY OF LONDON

(National Maritime Museum)

Again there is no mention of a valuation of the sailing vessels SUPERIOR (1814), FLORENCE (1831), ABERDONIAN (1) (1840) or LONDON (1840) so presumably their value had been written down to zero.

On 29th March 1847 the newly built DUKE OF SUTHERLAND arrived at Aberdeen from the Clyde and on 1st April she replaced NORTH STAR on the Inverness sailings. Because of her draft she was found unable to enter Burghead, and at times she had difficulty in berthing at Inverness, so was soon withdrawn from the route. DUKE OF SUTHERLAND was also to be very tender and she had to be towed back to her builders on the Clyde for this fault to be corrected. She did not return to service until July 1847. In August 1847 the Company considered putting her up for sale at a price of £30,000 - nothing became of this idea.

DUKE OF SUTHERLAND only served the Company for a short time. She had sailed from London on 30th March 1853 with 25 passengers and when just north of the entrance to the Firth of Forth ran into a heavy south-westerly gale. On arriving off Aberdeen early on 1st April it was low water, so she had to drop anchor until late in the afternoon, when even though the conditions on the bar were confused, she raised anchor and proceeded to enter harbour. Despite the fact that there were six men at the wheel, she was driven off course when struck by a heavy sea and driven on to the North Pier. Holed amidships and her engine room flooded, she drifted on to rocks and started to break up. A lifeboat was somehow launched and eight men and one woman eventually were washed up on the beach in her, but 16 persons died.

The slightly larger EARL OF ABERDEEN arrived at Aberdeen from her builders on 16th July 1847 and the fleet stabilised at five steamers. No changes in the fleet took place until April 1850, when the 21 year old wooden paddle steamer DUKE OF WELLINGTON was broken up. Between the period June and December 1851 the steamers carried 1,605 1st cabin and 1,222 2nd-cabin passengers. Passengers had to pay for their meals on board, with the charges for 1st cabin being Breakfast 1/6d (13p), Lunch 1/- (5p), Plain Tea 1/-, and a Cup of Tea or Coffee 6d (3p), whilst those in 2nd-cabin were 1/-, 9d, 10d and 4d respectively.

PADDLE TO SCREW

The result of competition from the railways and the loss of DUKE OF SUTHERLAND caused the Annual General Meeting in 1853 to vote to withdraw from the Inverness route, although this was against the recommendations of the management committee. This withdrawal opened the opportunity for the Edinburgh-based North of Scotland Steam Packet Company to run a service from Granton, near Edinburgh, to Inverness and their iron paddle steamer MARTELLO (483/43) was placed on the route. In June 1857 the Company resumed sailings to Inverness and Invergordon, taking the place of the Aberdeen, Leith & Clyde Shipping Company's steamer which had been withdrawn from the route, with their new iron screw steamer DUCHESS OF ROTHESAY. Built by William Denny & Brothers of Dumbarton, she was the Company's first iron screw steamer. The 23 year-old wooden paddle steamer CITY OF ABERDEEN (1) was "traded-in" for £4,000 as part payment for the new ship.

NORTH STAR was sold to Dundee owners in early 1853 and the insured value of the Company's property at the end of December 1853 was £30,000 for the nine year-old CITY OF LONDON (1), £21,000 for the six year old EARL OF ABERDEEN, £10,000 for the 18 year old CITY OF ABERDEEN (1), £3,983 for the Wharf at London and £1,500 for Waterloo Quay, Aberdeen.

By 1854 there were no longer any sailing vessels in the fleet and the service to Hull had been discontinued. FLORENCE (1831) had been sold in July 1849, LONDON (1840) had been lost at sea in February 1850, SUPERIOR (1814) had been sold in October 1852, and the sale of PARAGON (1842), ABERDONIAN (1)(1840) and GAZELLE (1846), the latter having been sailed out to Australia, followed in the summer of 1853.

The capital stock of the Company was reduced in 1853 to £80,000 and at the same time profits dropped. This reduction in capital could be put down to the fact that the railways had arrived at Aberdeen from the south in 1850 and this undoubtedly caused a drop in traffic To offset this competition, the Company came to terms with the railway companies to offer through rates for cattle to Manchester via Hull. By 1856 they also reached agreement as regards the proportion of livestock traffic carried by sea and rail from Aberdeen to London, but this arrangement was not renewed after 1859. Despite this competition, the price charged to carry cattle from Aberdeen to London by sea remained fairly constant, with the cost in 1839 being 25/- (£1.25), in 1844 from 22/6d to 27/6d (£1.12 to £1.25), rising in 1850 to 60/- (£3.00), before the intervention of the railways when the price fell back again to 25/- (£1.25) - in some ways the easier movement of livestock by rail to Aberdeen seems to have stimulated sea traffic The main movement of livestock from the north to the south took place between October and March/April each year, requiring on occasions a second steamer to back-up the advertised departures. In the summer, however the non-passenger carrying steamers were often laid-up, rather the reverse of other coastal shipping companies, who had to find extra vessels to meet the summer passenger trade. However, it was Company policy to have a skeleton crew on board the laid-up vessel, normally made up of a master, two mates, a chief engineer and a carpenter, so that should one of the regular vessels suffer a mishap or be severely delayed by bad weather coming North, the laid-up vessel could be brought into service in a relatively short time, and the advertised sailings maintained.

Over the years the registered owners and principal shareholders of the Company changed. In July 1855 they were James Sims, Alexander B.White, Alexander Anderson and Alexander Jopp. Some four years later they were Benjamin Moir, William Hogarth, Henry C.Oswald and Captain John Cargill. By June 1862 they were Alexander Eddie, John Stewart, Henry C.Oswald and Captain John Cargill.

CHARTERS

When trading activities were depressed, the Company would charter out its vessels to other owners. In 1836 some of its sailing ships had been chartered to Dundee shipowners. BON ACCORD, was eventually sold to owners of that port in July 1840. NORTH STAR was chartered in 1845 to the Peninsular & Oriental Steam Navigation Company of London for a period, as was CITY OF LONDON (1) in 1852, when she was chartered to operate between Marseilles and Malta or Southampton and Constantinople for six months at a rate of £170 per week (plus costs and insurance) - she was subsequently chartered for a further four months at £200 per week. CITY OF ABERDEEN (1) was chartered to Gee & Company of Hull (they had bought QUEEN OF SCOTLAND some six years earlier) for a period of six months from April 1849 at a rate of £150 per week for service between Hull, Hamburg and St Petersburg. In 1850 NORTH STAR was chartered to carry cattle from Tonning, Schleswig Holstein to London at £400 per voyage. In 1851 she was employed between the Humber and the Elbe at £90 per week, and in 1852 took 200 head of cattle from Southampton to Oporto for the sum of £600. None of her charters proved profitable because of expenses incurred in repairs to her engine and damage suffered in the course of her trading. NORTH STAR was sold to Dundee owners in June 1853, who having unshipped her engines, sailed her out to Australia, refitted the engines and sold her to Melbourne owners.

In May 1853 the Board discussed whether it would be prudent to charter vessels whilst retaining just two for the London sailings, with no *spare* available to meet unforeseen mishaps or delays. As the Dundee, Perth & London Shipping Company, as well as other companies operating out of Leith, worked their sailings to London on this basis, it was decided that charters could be accepted. In July 1853 an approach was made by the Peninsular & Oriental Steam Navigation Company of London to charter CITY OF LONDON (1) for four months at £200 per month. This offer was originally refused but subsequently a three month charter at £170 per month was agreed from 16th August. She sailed from Southampton on 20th with mails for Gibraltar. When the charter expired in November, it was extended for a further month at a rate of £190 per month, being then further extended in December to January 1854 at a rate of £220 per month. The charter finally terminated on 12th January 1854. The charterers offered to buy CITY OF LONDON (1) for £30,000 but this the Company declined. With British forces now involved in the Crimea, in February 1854 CITY OF LONDON (1) was chartered by the British Government for use in the Crimean War at a rate of £600 per week, coal being supplied by the charterer. Her crew, whilst lying in the River Thames in anticipation of this charter being taken up, included the master, three mates, a carpenter, 15 able-bodied seamen, two ordinary seamen, a cook, a steward, three boys, 18 firemen and a clerk. There was also a Stewardess on board, but she was discharged before sailing from the Thames, and entrusted with the return to Aberdeen of all curtains on the ship - obviously the military personnel were not going to be provided with such luxury as these items ! Whilst employed principally between Malta and Gibraltar, on 14th November 1854 she was anchored off Balaclava when a severe gale hit the area. Many ships lying off the port were driven ashore and wrecked but Captain John Cargill managed to extricate his ship from the chaos around him, but in doing so had a slip an anchor and 90 fathoms of chain. CITY OF LONDON (1) returned from Malta in need of a new boiler in February 1855, and arrived at Granton for this work to be carried out. She sailed from Granton on 20th March 1855 for London to load military supplies at Deptford for the Black Sea once more. She was then mainly employed carrying horses and cattle from Genoa and Malta to Balaclava. In July 1855 she again developed boiler trouble and had to be towed into Gibraltar Bay, where she remained for 18 days whilst repairs were made. Then employed sailing between Leghorn and Constantinople until she sailed from Malta for the last time on 21st September 1856 and arrived at Liverpool on 8th October, after which she sailed for Aberdeen. CITY OF ABERDEEN (1) was also chartered to the British Government for service in the Crimea in March 1855 for four months at 55/- (£2.75) per ton carried per month. EARL OF ABERDEEN (1) was chartered by the British Government, sailing from Portsmouth on 30th May 1854. She had a very bad passage to Gibraltar and there was some doubt whether she was suitable for the Bay of Biscay during the winter months. She then proceeded to Malta and Alexandria before returning to Liverpool in November 1854. However, a six month charter was signed on 26th July 1855 and she did not finally return to Aberdeen until the following February. For a short period in 1855 all three steamers in the fleet were on charter. In 1855 revenue from charters amounted to £27,824 out of total receipts of £30,160, thus providing some 92% of the total revenue for that year, compared with just over 35% in 1845 before passing the 86% mark in 1854.

Whilst the regular steamers were on charter providing the Company with a good return, it was necessary for the Company itself to charter or purchase ships to maintain the London sailings. In September 1854, while CITY OF LONDON (1) was away on charter, the iron screw steamer CANDIDATE (584/54) of London was chartered on 2nd October at £60 per week for four months to fill the gap. However, CANDIDATE was soon found to be unsuitable for the trade and was released in January 1855. The revenues received from the Government charters also allowed the Company to consider the purchase of steamers in place of the vessels on charter. In January 1855 the wooden paddle steamers ROYAL VICTORIA (1835) and the slightly smaller ROYAL ADELAIDE (1832), both owned by the London, Leith, Edinburgh & Glasgow Shipping Company were examined with the possibility of purchasing either or both of them. ROYAL ADELAIDE was chartered for one month to ascertain whether she might be suitable, but she was considered under-powered, and although an offer to take her up on a short two month charter at £140 per week was made, she was finally turned down as unsuitable. ROYAL VICTORIA had been advertised for sale in January 1855 for £7,000. The Company made an offer of £4,500 for her, and finally her owners compromised in March 1855 at a sum of £4,800. Two Liverpool-registered vessels were also considered, the wooden paddle steamer COMMODORE (1838), lying at Glasgow on offer at £13,500, and the iron paddle steamer TYNWALD (1846). The latter was found unsuitable for the trade so the former was purchased instead, but at a reduced price of £10,000. She sailed from Glasgow for Aberdeen on 21st April 1855 and took up the sailings of EARL OF ABERDEEN which had recently been taken up on British Government charter. In April 1855 ROYAL VICTORIA took up the London sailings, but in October 1855 on the return of CITY OF LONDON (1) from the Black Sea, she was chartered to the North of Europe Steam Shipping Company to make two voyages between Tonning, Schleswig-Holstein and Lowestoft. In July 1856 she was chartered for two voyages to Lisbon for a sum of £900. She served the Company for just short of two years before being sold for breaking up in November 1856. When all the regular steamers had returned from the Black Sea, there was no requirement for her, and from September 1856 twice weekly sailings to London were maintained by CITY OF ABERDEEN (1), CITY OF LONDON (1) and EARL OF ABERDEEN.

An unusual reason for delays in the sailings came to the fore in February 1855. It had been a severe winter and the River Thames became frozen. Subsequently when the thaw set in large lumps of ice drifted down the river and both EARL OF ABERDEEN and ROYAL VICTORIA were damaged whilst lying at the Wapping berth.

CRISIS AND COMPETITION

The starboard engine of COMMODORE failed on 9th April 1856, when she was 20 miles south of Flamborough Head, Yorkshire, on passage to London, but she continued her voyage on one engine and duly arrived at Gravesend. She later had to proceed to Glasgow for repairs. In 1856 she re-opened the Aberdeen to Inverness sailings, now no longer being required on the London sailings. Subsequently she was withdrawn from that route and chartered to the North of Scotland, Orkney & Shetland Steam Navigation Company to sail between Leith and Lerwick/Inverness during the winter of 1857/58 as a substitute for their steamer QUEEN, which had recently been lost.

After the mid-1850s the importance of chartering to the Company's finances diminished and in turn during the 1860s and 1870s the Company itself was compelled to charter ships from other owners to meet short term trading demands. The Company decided the time had come to introduce screw steamers to their sailings and in March 1857 William Denny & Brothers of Dumbarton delivered the iron screw steamer DUKE OF ROTHESAY which allowed the Inverness sailings to be re-opened. On the sale of CITY OF ABERDEEN (1) in January 1858, it was found necessary in the early part of 1858 to charter the Aberdeen, Leith & Clyde Shipping Company's wooden paddle steamer DUKE OF RICHMOND (1838) for some months, in order to maintain a twice weekly London service. In turn COMMODORE was chartered to the Aberdeen, Leith & Clyde Shipping Company during the summers of 1857 and 1858.

With the Company in 1858 then owning four steamers, the iron paddle steamers CITY OF LONDON (1844), EARL OF ABERDEEN (1847), the iron screw DUKE OF ROTHESAY (1857), and the wooden paddle steamer COMMODORE (1838), it was decided that the share capital could be reduced to a sum of £50,000.

The year 1859 saw the departure of two ships from the fleet - one intentional, the other unexpected. Traffic on the Inverness sailings had proved from its re-introduction in 1857 not to be profitable, with serious competition coming from the North of Scotland Steam Packet Company's vessels, who first introduced sailings between Granton to Inverness in 1853. DUKE OF ROTHESAY had been chartered for this reason to the North of Scotland, Orkney & Shetland Steam Navigation Company to operate between Leith and Inverness in the summer of 1858, and again in the Spring of 1859 for three months to a company trading as the Inverness & Edinburgh Steam Packet Company. She was sold (advertised sale price £27,000) to the Spanish Government for £14,000, having been on charter to them since 1st June, and handed over at Cadiz in July 1859. COMMODORE, once again on charter to the Aberdeen, Leith & Clyde Shipping Company, had the misfortune to be wrecked off the Fife coast on 16th September 1859. Suddenly the Company found itself with just two steamers, and no back-up. Even when the North of Scotland Steam Packet Company's MARTELLO was lost in November 1857, she had been replaced by the iron screw steamer DUNKELD (525/44) and competition on the route continued to be fierce. This company eventually withdrew its service in 1864, leaving the Aberdeen, Leith & Clyde Shipping Company to maintain the service alone.

In December 1859 serious competition appeared on the London sailings when a service was introduced from adjacent berth 74 Waterloo Quay to Newcastle Steam Wharf, Wapping by John Stewart of Aberdeen trading as the Northern Steam Navigation

Company - this title became just the Northern Steam Company in May 1860. Two screw steamers were employed on this service by 1861, GAMBIA, backed-up by the London registered steamer KANGAROO (458/53) - whether the latter vessel was on charter or as part of a partnership is not quite clear (for the record she is shown in the Fleet List as No. 12A), being registered in the ownership of David Dunn, the manager of the Northern Steam Navigation Company. Subsequently KANGAROO was replaced in January 1861 on the purchase of STANLEY. Such was the competition that by February 1860 only a weekly sailing was being provided by EARL OF ABERDEEN, a Wednesday sailing out of Aberdeen, and a Saturday one from London. Passenger single fares had by this time dropped to just £1 for the 1st-cabin and 12-6d (60p) for 2nd-cabin. This situation was resolved in October 1861 when the Company first chartered the opposition's vessels, subsequently buying them, so bringing their fleet up to four vessels. GAMBIA was incorporated into the Company's sailing list on 2nd November 1861, when she sailed from London for Aberdeen. STANLEY was placed on various charters and February 1862 found herself in the Adriatic calling at Trieste and Venice, and in October 1862 was at Nassau.

The iron paddler EARL OF ABERDEEN (1), now some 16 years old and requiring repairs and new boilers which would have cost £10,000, was sold in April 1863 to London owners (probably for use as a livestock hulk), leaving CITY OF LONDON (1) and GAMBIA to maintain the London sailings, with STANLEY at that time laid-up. CITY OF LONDON (1) was in May 1864 fitted with a new boiler and also her paddle feathering renewed at great expense, but she was not considered satisfactory, so was sent round to her builders yard on the Clyde for a further inspection in September 1864. During this period STANLEY was brought out of her lay-up berth and joined GAMBIA on the London sailings.

From time to time the Company were requested to transport horses and carriages from London to Balmoral when Queen Victoria was in residence there. This called for an extra steamer, so when such a request was received in October 1864 for her horses and carriages to be shipped back to London at the end of her summer visit to Balmoral, the Company had no other option but to nominate GAMBIA for the task. With no spare vessel available, they were forced to go out to charter. Worse was to follow, on 24th November 1864 STANLEY was wrecked off Tynemouth, leaving the Company with just one serviceable vessel. A charter was immediately arranged with Thos. Wilson, Son & Company of Hull to make available their steamer ARGO (778/60), but she developed engine problems. The steamer SENTINEL (551/60) of Newcastle was substituted in her place. An urgent request was made to Robert Napier & Company to return CITY OF LONDON (1), still under repair on the Clyde, but the completion of repairs was still sometime away.

GAMBIA struggled on by herself but in December 1864 while on passage from London to Aberdeen, the steam feed pipe to the engine failed and she had to put into Granton for emergency repairs. The Company hurriedly chartered the Leith, Hull & Hamburg Steam Packet Company's steamer BERLIN (651/63) for a month until GAMBIA was serviceable again.

CITY OF LONDON (1) after repairs costing £4,690, eventually sailed from the Clyde in February 1865 but as she was steaming off the Mull of Kintyre (at the exit from the Firth of Clyde), a crack in the hull was observed so she had to return to Napier's yard. This repaired, she arrived back at Aberdeen but it was obvious that her days with the fleet were numbered. When the bill for the repairs was received, it was fiercely disputed by the Company, especially as the boiler was still not completely satisfactory. CITY OF LONDON (1) managed to bring Queen Victoria's horses and carriages back up North again in June 1865. On 24th July 1866 while on passage from Aberdeen to London, the shaft of her starboard engine broke when off Cromer, Norfolk. Her place on the sailings was taken by the steamer OSSIAN (725/55) chartered from the London & Edinburgh Shipping Company of Leith. The shaft for the port engine had to be replaced in October 1866.

EXPANSION

It was not until 1865 that a additional steamer came into service. This was an iron screw steamer built at Port Glasgow by R. Duncan & Company at a cost of £20,600. She was named CITY OF ABERDEEN (2) on being launched in October 1865. She arrived at Aberdeen on 13th November 1865, with her maiden voyage commencing from Aberdeen on 18th November. On her trials she had reached a speed of nearly 14 knots and had accommodation for 60 1st-class and 30 2nd-class passengers. She was not to prove a very satisfactory ship, suffering from boiler problems right from the start of her service. With now both CITY OF LONDON (1) and CITY OF ABERDEEN (2) available for service, during the summer months of 1867 GAMBIA was put out to charter and in June of that year loaded a cargo of salted herring at Stornoway for Stettin. During the summer of 1869 she was the spare vessel and laid-up at Aberdeen.

With traffic increasing and the frequent need to supplement the regular steamer with a back-up vessel, the decision was made to expand the fleet and a new building programme was started. An order was placed in 1869 with John Elder & Company of Glasgow for an iron screw passenger steamer costing £28,500, and BAN-RIGH was delivered in the spring of 1870.

However, before the new vessel could join the fleet GAMBIA was lost. She foundered in a gale about 4.0 a.m. on the morning of 7th January 1870 near the Dudgeon light vessel in the North Sea while on passage from London to Aberdeen, with a light general cargo of 87 tons, a crew of 29, and 25 passengers (of which 19 were seafarers). When just North of the Dudgeon light vessel at 12.15 a.m., the chief engineer reported a leak in the after

BAN-RIGH   *(Ambrose Greenway collection)*

part through the shaft tunnel, and although the pumps were set in motion and the crew and passengers employed in baling out the water with buckets, the water gained quickly. The vessel was turned to head for the Humber but on the boiler fires being put out by the rising water, the vessel came to a stop and began to sink rapidly. Distress rocks were fired and blue lights burnt, and although a steamer and a sailing vessel were nearby, neither responded to the call for help. The crew and passengers took to three boats at 2.30 a.m. and it was not until six hours later that they were picked up by the Russian barque SOLON and landed on the 8th at North Shields. A Court of Enquiry was set up at the Sheriff Court House, Aberdeen on 31st January 1870 into the loss, but it came up with no firm conclusion as to why GAMBIA had foundered.

A replacement for CITY OF LONDON (1), the last of the iron paddle steamers which had been converted to screw propulsion in 1869, was decided upon in July 1870 and a further order was given to John Elder & Company, Glasgow in August for an iron screw vessel costing £32,000. CITY OF LONDON (2) although not having a clipper bow, had a yacht like appearance. On delivery of the new vessel in June 1871, the older vessel of the same name was sold to London owners for £3,935. Unfortunately, in January 1871 CITY OF ABERDEEN (2)(1865) was wrecked just south of Aberdeen due to a navigational error, so the Dundee, Perth & London Shipping Company's steamer LONDON (622/56) was

23

chartered to fill the gap. A search was made to try and obtain a spare vessel and although Michael Langlands & Son's steamer PRINCESS ROYAL (566/63), on the market for £17,500, and the J & G. Burns steamer PENGUIN (518/64), on the market for £15,000, were inspected at Glasgow in April 1871, neither were found acceptable.

CITY OF LONDON (2) and BAN-RIGH maintained Wednesday and Saturday sailings, relieved by the charter of the North of Scotland, Orkney & Shetlands Steam Navigation Company's QUEEN (413/61) from time to time, when either of the two steamers were slipped on the gridiron or went into the Victoria Graving Dock in London. It was not until April 1872 that the Port Glasgow shipbuilders Cunliffe & Dunlop were given an order for a sister ship to CITY OF LONDON (2). CITY OF ABERDEEN (3), costing £40,000, was completed in the Spring of 1873, which then brought the fleet back to three.

RE-ORGANISATION

The Company became a limited liability company, as recognised under The Companies Act 1862 and 1867, on 14th April 1875 with capital of £75,000 in shares of £1/5s/0d. (£1.25), purchasing the old company's assets valued at £90,000, incorporating the North of Scotland Steam Navigation Company at a valued of £30,000. The principal shareholders were Thomas Adam, banker (225), Alexander P. Hogarth, merchant (2,500), Hugh Hogarth, merchant (2,481), and John Stewart, manufacturer (5,000), all of Aberdeen, plus 792 smaller shareholders. The capital was increased to £100,000 on 19th July 1877.

The amount of cargo being carried annually was expanding, having risen from some 26,500 tons in 1862, to nearly 31,000 tons by 1865, and reaching just over 50,000 tons by 1875. Passenger fares in 1875 were still quite reasonable and a private cabin (sleeping four persons) cost £6/0/0d single, whilst a return 1st cabin cost 30/- (£1.50) and 2nd cabin 15/- (£0.75p) - return fares were 45/- and 25/- (£2.25 and £1.25) respectively, included the steward's fee and provisions. In 1860 the fares were £1/0/0d for the Main cabin and 12/6d (£0.65) for 2nd. Going back to September 1827 the cabin fare was £5-0-0d, whilst steerage cost £2/10s/0d. (£2.50) so basically travel had become cheaper over some 40 years.

On 1st April 1875 the Company opened a new wharf on the Thames, and some two years later took delivery of the new iron screw tug ICH DIEN. With movement on the Thames increasing there was a need to provide a tug to turn the steamers in the river, move lighters from one berth to another, and at times convey passengers from the ship up-river to Temple Pier, when tides prevented the steamers going alongside the wharf immediately on arrival. On the occasions when staff had their annual summer outing on the Thames, the Company charged just £2 for its use!

ICH DIEN (German for "I Serve") was to perform all these functions for the Company over the next 67 years.

ICH DIEN on a staff outing on the River Thames.   *(National Maritime Museum)*

With the heavy demand for the carriage of livestock south in the winter months of 1896, the Company considered acquiring an extra steamer which could supplement the London service when required, and also operate into Moray Firth ports when cargo inducement called for such a call.   The purchase of the British & Irish Steam Packet Company's COUNTESS OF DUBLIN (760/69) for £16,500 was considered in February 1876, but this was rejected and instead an order for a   new steamer, somewhat smaller than previous vessels, was placed.   She was named HOGARTH and again built by Cunliffe & Dunlop, coming into service in the winter of 1876.   She only served the Company for less than two years as the trade for which she had been built had not come up to expectations, so she was chartered in June 1878 to the London & South Western Railway Company of Southampton for service to Jersey and St Malo, France.   The charterers subsequently bought the vessel (with delivery at Southampton) for £16,500 some two months later.

At the end of November 1878 BAN-RIGH suffered severe boiler problems and the "North Company's" steamer QUEEN had once again to be chartered to replace her. She was in service for three and a half weeks, which cost the Company £303. However, by February 1879 traffic was so poor that BAN-RIGH was laid-up. The revenue received from the carriage of passengers and cargo had risen sharply from £39,163 in 1870 to £50,600 by 1875. Revenue had risen still further in 1876 to £54,140, in 1877 to £56,750 when thrice weekly sailings were operated, but in 1878 when sailings were once again reduced to twice weekly, revenue dropping to £55,300 and by 1879 was down to £52,037. By March 1881, however, traffic had once more recovered necessitating the chartering of the Aberdeen steamer HAYLE (373/67) at £150 per week to back-up some of the regular sailings for a short period. By January 1882 three regular sailings per week were again being operated.

Technology was catching up with the Company too, as in September 1881 the office had its first telephone installed ! Further innovations took place in November 1886 when CITY OF LONDON (2) was fitted with electricity at a cost of £1,130 - the other ships in the fleet were similarly fitted in 1887.

The sailings to Inverness had continued to be operated as and when trade demanded, using chartered tonnage. However, in April 1881 Cunliffe & Dunlop was given an order for a small steamer, costing £12,560, for specific employment on the Moray Firth sailings. HARLAW (2) was launched on 14th October 1881, arrived at Aberdeen on 19th November, and commenced sailings to the Moray Firth ports. Although initially traffic was good, serious competition appeared on the route in 1882 from the newly formed Aberdeen, Leith & Moray Firth Steamship Company. The Company withdrew soon afterwards from the Inverness route, and never resumed sailings on that route again. HARLAW (1) was unsuitable to serve on the London sailings, being too small, so filled-in wherever she could or was put out to charter, including a spell of two months running between Liverpool and Jersey in May 1882. In April 1888 the vessel was sold for £5,000 to Newfoundland owners, who sailed her across the Atlantic for a new life in Canadian waters.

FROM IRON TO STEEL

In anticipation of monies to be received from the sale of HARLAW (1), an order had been placed with the local shipbuilding yard of Hall, Russell & Company (the first steamer to be built for the Company at an Aberdeen yard since 1829) for the Company's first steel screw steamer, and also the first in the fleet fitted with a triple expansion engine. Launched on 21st October 1887 as OITHONA, she took up service at the end of 1887 but her time with the Company was to be short, as when the opportunity arose to sell her for £16,000 (just £350 less than she cost originally) to the Russian Imperial Navy in September 1891, this was taken up. She was sent to the yard of R. Craggs & Company, Middlesbrough where she was converted to a despatch vessel. Renamed YACOUT in February 1892, on her trials she exceeded a speed of 13 knots. There were no further reports

of her movements until she arrived at Bizerta, Tunisia in January 1921
as part of the Russian Wrangell Squadron bringing the remains of the
defeated White Russian Army out of the Crimea. General Pyotr N.
Wrangel (born 1878, died 1928) was of Baltic German nobleship; and
joined the Russian Volunteer (White) Army in August 1918 to fight the
Bolsheviks (the Red Communist Army which had come into being in
November 1917). General Wrangell had become the Commander-in
Chief of the Armed Forces in the south of Russia on 4th April 1920 and
remained so until 13th November 1920. After the White Army was
driven from Roskov and had retired to the Crimea, it was dissolved on
13th November 1920 after its defeat by the Red Army. Some 140,000
men, women and children were evacuated on a fleet of small vessels
to become refugees in Bulgaria, Serbia, Greece, Prinkipo, Lemnos,
Egypt, and Tunisia. Carrying a contingent of these refugees was
YACOUT. In 1923, being of no further use to the refugees, the vessel
was sold to Maltese owners and renamed G M LA VALETTE, then in
1926 to Tunisian owners, before becoming the Greek owned IONION
in 1934. She remained in service until 1937 when she was broken up
in Italy - a creditable service afloat of 50 years.

At the annual valuation of the fleet at the end of 1887, the vessels
were valued at :

BAN-RIGH	17 years old	£22,000
CITY OF LONDON (2)	16 years old	£21,400
CITY OF ABERDEEN (3)	14 years old	£27,400
ICH DIEN	10 years old	£ 2,200
HARLAW (1)	6 years old	£ 8,450
OITHONA	2 years old	£16,900

On 19th June 1891 BAN-RIGH undertook a cruise to the North
Cape, Norway and Lapland. The number of passengers was limited
to 45 with the fare being just £35 or £30, depending on
accommodation. The North of Scotland, Orkney & Shetland Steam
Navigation Company had been operating cruises from Aberdeen to
Norway for some years previously, immediately protested strongly
at this intrusion into their trade, and the experiment was not
repeated again.

A fourth passenger steamer was ordered in February 1892 at a cost
of £37,600. HOGARTH (2) was handed over by Hall, Russell &
Company in January 1893 and was the largest steamer owned to date.
During the summer of 1893 only two steamers were employed on the
sailings, HOGARTH (2) and BAN-RIGH, with CITY OF LONDON (2) and
CITY OF ABERDEEN (3) being laid-up or available as back-up vessel.
However, in June and July 1896 a backlog of cargo developed
(presumably there had been a bumper harvest and grain was coming
forward earlier than expected) so the local cargo steamer GLEN TILT
(666/83) was chartered for two months. This situation was further
complicated in August 1896 on the placing of two small steamers,
BALGAY (229/95) and RINGMOOR (257/89), on sailings to London by
other local interests. The agent for this operation was William R. Aiken
of 53 Regent Quay, but this competition only survived a short time.

HOGARTH (2) outward bound on the River Thames.   *(Graeme Somner collection)*

A PASSENGER'S OUTLOOK

As an illustration of the standard of travel available in 1892, the following extract from a traveller's diary is of interest. The gentleman in question was travelling from London to Aberdeen in a four-berth cabin which, according to the sailing bills of that time, the cost being £6 each way (presumably his share of this sum being £1/10/- (£1.50)), plus the 1st cabin return ticket of 45/- (£2.25), which included his meals:

"31st July, 11 p.m. - Sunday at Sea.

When I woke on my little upper shelf, I threw open the "scuttle" of the private port-hole in my berth, and there was the blue sea, level as Salisbury Plain, stretching away into the distance and sparkling in the sunshine. At the sight of this beautiful marine vignette, framed by the brass rim of the "scuttle", I scrambled down from my elevated roost like a monkey, nearly breaking the neck of the man below, who was climbing out simultaneously like a mole. Soon I was on deck drinking in the fresh sea-breeze in great gulps. I felt I was living at last, and the dusty cobwebs of which my head seemed full when I left London were blown away in five minutes. You know I am not a good sailor, but the steamer was going as smoothly as a tramway car (without the bumps), and my appetite was as sharp as a razor. You may judge how impossible it was to have "mal de mer", when I tell you that I not only accepted but actually smoked, before breakfast, a cigar from an affable stranger who had just returned from the Ardennes, and had bought a hundred there for seven and sixpence. No land was to be seen, but it was understood that we were somewhere off the Wash, having passed Lowestoft and Yarmouth in the night; and one aspirating man said he had been up early enough to see Cromer. From that moment we all viewed him with aversion, for on board ship nobody should see more than anybody else.

Then the breakfast-bell rang, and we all rushed below with an ocean-hunger that must have appalled worthy John McIntosh, most genial of head-stewards, arrayed in spotless navy blue, who has held the keys of the cabin for some thirty-five years. Never had he been face to face with a more numerous and more voracious lot of passengers - but he was equal to the task.

BREAKFAST MENU - 9 a.m.

*Fresh Herring, Fried Soles, Fried Cod
Boiled Eggs, Mutton Chops
Beefsteak, Fried Sausages, Grilled Bacon
Stewed Kidneys, American Dry Hash
Cold Meats*

Toast and Preserves

---

*Hot Rolls,
Tea, Coffee, Cocoa*

Captain Chambers, who has been in the Company's service some sixteen years, sat at the head of the table - a fine type of sailor, and looking ornamental as well as useful in his navy blue uniform, with its gold braid and brass buttons. The long saloon is a bright and airy room, the light pouring down on the table from the deck saloon, a sort of covered galley overhead. As background to each row of breakfasting passengers are the state-rooms in light veneer, picked out with darker beads in the most cheerful and tasteful style of nautical upholstery; while, at the stern, the cabin widens out into a semi-circle Fortunately there is accommodation enough for us all.

By this time everybody knows everybody else, and we march up and down the deck in twos and threes, smoking and chatting. Beyond a slight tremor caused by the revolutions of the screw, and a gentle quiver and sway in the deck, as if it were a spring board, there is no movement on the vessel, yet we are cutting through the water at twelve and a half knots an hour, or say, 14 land miles. She is a good boat, the CITY OF LONDON, of 957 tons burden and 1,500 horse-power, 242 feet in length and thirty and a half feet in breadth. The Company has two similar boats, the *CITY OF ABERDEEN* and the *BAN-RIGH*, one of the three sailing from London and one from Aberdeen every Wednesday and Saturday throughout the year, and doing the trip either way in thirty-six hours. A fourth steamer is now building - one bigger than these - of 1,200 tons burden, 2,500 horse-power, 252 feet in length, and thirty-two and a half feet in breadth; she will be ready next year, and is to be called *HOGARTH*, after the Chairman of the Company.

CITY OF LONDON turning in the River Thames with the assistance of ICH DIEN.
(W.S.P.L.)

Everybody is on deck, for even the most lackadaisical intentions cannot make anybody ill in weather like this. The sea is like a lake, hardly a tuft of white to be seen. So calm and unbroken is the vast expanse of water, that it is a positive relief to go forward and watch our sharp stem cleaving the blue plain, and turning back the bubbling water like earth before a ploughshare. On each side the swell strikes out obliquely from our bow and dies gently away, while the flecks of foam float past the sides of the vessel. The only objects that break the monotony of the bare sea are the sails and hulls of shipping, now a three-master, or barque, or brig, or schooner (for we are soon very cunning in rigs), with her canvas shining white in the sun; now a steamer with the smoke streaming in an endless line from the smoke-stack. The favourite amusement is to count the sails visible; at first only half a dozen seem to be in sight, but the careful searcher can pick out thirty with the naked eye, and forty with a glass. Occasionally we pass a vessel quite close, and can't understand why our captain on the bridge does not grow excited like ourselves. Sometimes quite a procession of big steamers rush past, colliers returning from the "Wash". Presently land looms up ahead, and the sight could hardly excite more enthusiasm amongst a crowd of shipwrecked mariners on a raft. It is Flamborough Head, the first point we strike after leaving the Norfolk Coast, and it is "halfway-house" in our journey. A magnificent sight it is a mark the rugged front of Yorkshire thrusting out into the sea, the battered grey cliffs crowned by a verdant table-land, with a tall light-house at the edge. The incessant beating of the waves has worn the face of the crags into a honeycomb of caves and grottoes and isolated pinnacles, until the round of the cliff looks like a richly ornamented wedding cake. Had the weather been clear, we should have coasted along inshore, past Scarborough and Whitby, but a thick haze lies off the land, and the steamer has to keep out to sea. There is, therefore, no more land till we come to Aberdeen, but as a solace to our disappointment comes the dinner bell, summoning us to a substantial "table d'hote". At sea eating becomes a sacred duty, and not one of us is remiss.

DINNER MENU - 2 p.m.

Boiled Salmon and Cucumber

Roast Beef, Corned Beef
Boiled Mutton and Caper Sauce
Roast Lamb and Mint Sauce
Roast Duck, Boiled Fowl, Ox Tongue
Boiled Ham
Roast Mutton and Red Currant Jelly

Cauliflower, Green Peas

Plum Tart, Custard Pudding
Stewed Prunes and Rice
Apple Tart, Sago Pudding

Biscuits, Cheese, Salad

Strawberries and Cream
Grapes, Pears, Melon
Nuts, Assorted

Then up on deck again to watch the smooth sea, and the groups of sea parrots and divers floating about on the gentle swell, turning up their white tails as we approach and sinking like stones, not to reappear until the steamer is well our of the way. And what is that on the starboard quarter - that line of black bodies, sliding and curving through the water? The sea-serpent, say the imaginative ladies; a shoal of porpoises, say the practical gentlemen. But best of all it is to go amidships upon the bridge, and watch the jelly fish go by, churned up by the bow. They surge past in hundreds, glowing in the clear blue water like fragments of a rainbow that has foundered and broken up, their long feelers waving helplessly around them. They are very beautiful to look at, but a caution to meet in the water, for they sting like bunches of nettles, and stick to the skin like limpets. One passenger tells how he once dived from a boat off Scarborough, and drove his head right through a big one, and had to be rowed ashore blind and raving. On the forecastle the second class passengers are camped out, basking in the sun, an artistic touch of colour being given to the scene by the red coats of half a dozen soldiers, Highlanders home from Egypt, their bronzed faces looking grimly from beneath white helmets and puggrees.

At last the evening comes on, and the tea bell rings for us to assemble once more in the dining saloon.

TEA MENU - 7 p.m.

Finnan Haddock, Spiced Herring
Fried Skate, Fried Ling

———

Cold Meats, Roast Beef, Corned Beef
Boiled Mutton, Roast Lamb, Boiled Ham, Boiled Ox Tongue

———

Toast and Preserves

———

Tea, Coffee, Cocoa

After the meal, the passengers divide into three parties. One settles down in the cosy smoke-room on deck, with tumblers of "Special Scotch"; another betakes itself to the sofas in the deck saloon, and sings the liveliest hymns that can be found in the collection, to the accompaniment of the piano; and the third party promenades the poop, smoking vigorously under shelter of the awning, and the only sound, beyond the muffled music from the deck-saloon, is the whisper of the water as we rush through it, and the sharp ring of the patent log, as each quarter-knot is registered."

The writer of the diary returned to London on BAN-RIGH on 8th August 1892, after having toured the Highlands by train and coach (horse drawn, not motor of course). He was fortunate enough to have fine weather again on the southward passage, for which he rejoiced.

ACQUISITIONS AND SALES

In May 1899 the Company made an offer of £19,000 for the London steamer SPINDRIFT (708/89) but, when this was rejected, purchased for £10,500 the 11-year old cargo ship GOTHA from Goole owners and renamed her HARLAW (2) - she was to provide additional space for freight when demand was greatest, but had no passenger accommodation. Unfortunately, whilst on trials on 25th August after a refit and before coming into service, she ran ashore in the Pentland Firth during fog. She was subsequently salvaged by the East Coast Salvage Company and arrived back at Aberdeen for repair. This incident cost the Company £2,750 in salvage fees and repairs and resulting in her not coming into service until 30th October.

In May 1899 too, there was a possibility that BAN-RIGH, re-engined with a triple expansion engine in 1893, would be chartered for service in the Mediterranean but, when this prospect fell through, she was put on the sale list. She was subsequently taken on charter by the North of Scotland, Orkney & Shetland Steam Navigation Company for two months at a rate of £420 per month, but unfortunately, on her second voyage for them, she ran ashore at Cairnbulg Point, near Fraserburgh, and had to be hurriedly replaced by CITY OF ABERDEEN (3). When no offers had been received for her by the summer of 1901, the intention was to sell her for breaking up. However, in October 1901 an offer of £18,580 was received from a Colombian supporter of General Matos, an opponent of the Venezuelan Government lead by President Castro, to carry the General back to Venezuela with the intention of landing arms and ammunition in that country in support of the rebels. She arrived at Antwerp in September 1901, where after loading a cargo of arms (and a quantity of wine!), her originally crew having been paid off, she set sail for St Pierre, Martinique where she arrived on 28th November. The Venezuelan Government offered a reward of US$10,000 for her capture but, now named LIBERADOR, she cruised round the islands and somehow evaded this fate. It appears that little maintenance was carried out on deck or in the engine room, growth sprouted on her deck and the boilers became brine scaled. No landing was apparently ever made in Venezuela and the vessel passed into the possession of the Bolivian Government about 1902, so presumably the whole operation was a disaster. In 1904 she was renamed MARROQUIN, now registered at Cartagena, Venezuela.

When the North of Scotland, Orkney & Shetland Steam Navigation Company's ST ROGNVALD was lost in April 1900, the Company chartered EARL OF ABERDEEN to cover her sailings until a replacement was found.

On occasions vessels were employed on unusual sailings. One of these was on 8th June 1902 when HOGARTH (2), with passengers embarked at London, joined the Coronation Royal Naval Review at Spithead, and others on 10th, 11th and 12th July

ABERDONIAN (2) (1909-1946)

KOOLGA (1918-1946)

Water colours by D. McBain.

34

LOCHNAGAR (1930-1946)

HARLAW (3) (1929-1946)

(Aberdeen Maritime Museum)

1907, when HARLAW (2) ran trips out of Aberdeen round the Channel Fleet lying in Aberdeen Bay.

The capital of the Company was re-organised again in March 1905 (this had taken place previously in July 1877 when the sum had been raised to £100,000) and this was now increased to £120,000, with the principal shareholders being Thomas Adam, shipowner, Theodore Crombie, George Davidson, Alexander M.Ogston, Alexander C. Pirie, and William Tait, all manufacturers, and Alexander M.Williamson, advocate.

No further changes in the fleet took place until October 1906 when the 33-year old CITY OF ABERDEEN (3) was sold for £8,000 to Greek owners for service between Cyprus and Alexandria. She sailed from Aberdeen for the Tyne on 13th October 1906 now renamed SALAMIS. This reduced the fleet to three once again, the passenger ships CITY OF LONDON (2)(1871), and HOGARTH (2)(1893) and the cargo-only ship HARLAW (2)(1895).

When passenger traffic started to pick-up again a further passenger ship was considered, so tenders were asked for from a number of shipbuilders. The figures received by the Company varied greatly :

Hall, Russell & Company Ltd., Aberdeen	£43,000
A. Stephen & Sons Ltd., Glasgow	£51,500
John Brown & Company Ltd., Clydebank	£51,000
D.J. Dunlop & Company, Port Glasgow	£46,750
Fairfield Shipbuilding Company Ltd., Govan, Glasgow	£50,825
D & W. Henderson & Company Ltd., Glasgow	£39,800
A & J. Inglis Ltd., Glasgow	£53,375
Caledon Shipbuilding Company Ltd., Dundee	£44,300

The order went to the Clyde shipbuilders D & W. Henderson & Company Ltd. Completed in the spring of 1909, ABERDONIAN (2) was the largest and best equipped ship that the Company had owned, having accommodation for 100 1st-class and 200 2nd-class passengers, and capable of a service speed of 14 knots.

Unfortunately, on 6th January 1910 whilst bound for Aberdeen, ABERDONIAN (2) was involved in a collision off Orfordness, Suffolk with the London collier HOLMWOOD (1327/02), on passage from the Tyne to London with a cargo of coal. The collier was sunk and, at the subsequent Court of Enquiry, the collision was blamed on ABERDONIAN (2). The Company had to meet a bill of £14,820 as result. In the autumn of 1910 the cargo-only steamer HARLAW (2) was offered for sale at a price of £5,250. She was eventually purchased in December 1910 by London owners for £3,500.

The year 1912 was a most unsettling one for the Company due to circumstances beyond their control. In March there was a national coal miners strike and the Company suddenly found itself faced with just three week's supply of coal at Aberdeen. They were forced to

ABERDONIAN (2) entering Aberdeen Harbour.

purchase coal at great expense from any coal merchant willing to sell to them, but fortunately the strike was settled before coal became a real problem. In early May the Port of London dockers came out on strike and cargo on many sailings could not be discharged, and had to be brought back to Aberdeen. Livestock was unloaded by the Company's wharf supervisory staff. Eventually, on 22nd June strike breakers were brought in, and lived on the ships they were working on, so as to avoid the picket lines, enabling the vessels to maintain a reasonable service. Settlement of the strike was reached on 8th July 1912.

In May 1914 consideration was given to replacing the 43-year old CITY OF LONDON (2) with the purchase, at a bargain price of £10,000, of the Glasgow passenger steamer LILY (625/96), but the sale was never completed. CITY OF LONDON (2) was in fact to give the Company a further 17 years service before finally being sold.

CITY OF LONDON (2) berthed in the River Thames (with the Newcastle coaster GRASMERE (600/04) approaching the berth).

(Ambrose Greenway collection)

DISRUPTION OF WAR

When war was declared on 4th August 1914 the Company were operating three steamers on the London sailings, CITY OF LONDON (2)(1871), HOGARTH (2)(1893) and ABERDONIAN (2)(1909). Because the vessels were not insured against War Risks, the Company immediately withdrew the prestigious ABERDONIAN (2) from service on 7th August and laid her up. HOGARTH (2) sailed from

London on the 8th and on her arrival in Aberdeen she too was laid-up. CITY OF ABERDEEN (2), however, sailed for London on the 9th but on her return to Aberdeen on the 14th was then laid-up. On 21st August CITY OF LONDON (2) and HOGARTH (2) were covered against war risks in the sums of £22,000 and £8,000 respectively and restarted the sailings. For a period the Company chartered the Aberdeen steamer BRAENEIL (424/12) to supplement the two regular steamers. When CITY OF LONDON (2) broke down in December 1914, ABERDONIAN (2) had to be brought into service, so cover for the sum of £40,000 against war risks was taken out.

In early 1915 ABERDONIAN (2) was hired as a hospital carrier by the Director of Military Sea Transport and despatched to the Mediterranean. On 14th February 1916 she sailed from Alexandria bound for Southampton for conversion to a recognised hospital ship. In April 1917, because of attacks on fully painted hospital ships, she was painted grey once more and was designated as an ambulance transport. She was handed back to the Company at Southampton in May 1919.

ABERDONIAN (2) as a Hospital Ship in World War 1.   *(Graeme Somner collection)*

This just left two ships to maintain the sailings. When sinkings in the North Sea became very serious in May 1917, the authorities initially ruled that ships could no longer sail independently, but had to wait for a convoy. To liner companies, this was very restrictive causing considerable delays in turn-rounds. However, in June 1917 HOGARTH (2) was fitted with a defensive gun, after which the authorities ruled that any vessel fitted with a gun could once again proceed independently. Unfortunately, HOGARTH (2) was torpedoed and sunk off the Farne Islands in June 1918. One survivor was picked up by a trawler and landed in the Tyne, after having drifted on a raft for nearly two days, but 26 other crew were lost, including the master. To replace this loss, the Company purchased in December 1918 the eight year-old cargo-only steamer KOOLGA from Leith owners. KOOLGA had been offered for sale at a price of £65,000 in October 1918 but by the time a decision had been made to buy her in November the price had risen to £69,000.

In August 1917 CITY OF LONDON (2) was chartered by Charles Mauritzen of Leith for two months to operate to Iceland, and in August 1918 she was chartered to Carron Company of Grangemouth for a sum of £2,500 per month, and sailed between Grangemouth and London until January 1919. As HOGARTH (2) had been sunk in June of that year, it would appear the Company withdrew from the London sailings from mid-1918.

In November 1918 The Aberdeen Steam Navigation Company was incorporated as a limited liability company. On return of peace (the word "The" was now officially part of the title), conditions in the coastal trades had changed dramatically, with most of the passenger traffic now moving by rail rather than sea.

KOOLGA arrived at London on her first sailing south on 8th January 1919. ABERDONIAN (2) was handed back to the Company at Southampton in May 1919 after over four years' service as a hospital ship and arrived back at Aberdeen on 26th May. She needed to be refurbished and her passenger accommodation was reduced from 100 to 80 1st class and 200 to 120 2nd class to meet the change in demand. The total cost of the work came to £21,939, this sum being re-imbursed to the Company by the Government. She resumed the London sailings on 10th September 1919. CITY OF LONDON (2) again took up the sailings from the beginning of June 1919, twice weekly departures then being maintained by the two passengers steamers, whilst KOOLGA provided supplementary capacity as required. KOOLGA was chartered in October 1919 to make a voyage from Peterhead to Hamburg, but unfortunately on her way north to Peterhead from London on 30th October she stripped all her propeller blades when south of Flamborough Head and had to be towed into Grimsby by the trawler EARL GRANARD (211/04) of Grimsby. She could not undertake her charter from Peterhead but instead, after repairs at Leith, she was chartered for six months by Whimster & Son of Glasgow (at £3,750 per month) to sail between Glasgow, Gibraltar and Genoa. The charter was subsequently extended for a further six months, so it was not until 22nd November 1920 that KOOLGA returned to the London sailings.

In August 1920 both ABERDONIAN (2) and CITY OF LONDON (2) were fitted with wireless telegraphy. CITY OF LONDON (2) was at the same time taken in hand by Hall, Russell & Company for extensive refurbishment - she was after all now nearly 50 years old, but this was the cheaper option instead of building a new steamer. The repairs cost £32,723 and she was back in service

KOOLGA at Newcastle Quay on 14th September 1946.

again on 28th April 1921.

As was 1912, the year 1921 was plagued with industrial problems. First in April London, dockers withdrew their labour and this was followed in May by a shortage of coal. It was found difficult to operate a twice-weekly service, so in June this was reduced to one passenger steamer sailing per week, with many sailings having to be cancelled during July, August and September. To get over the coal shortage, it was at one time suggested that KOOLGA be sent over to Antwerp to pick up a cargo of coal, but she was not really suitable for the carriage of such a cargo, so the Company had to live from hand to mouth by buying coal from where they could, until the mines were able to produce the tonnages required.

At the annual valuation of the fleet in December 1924 , the value of the vessels was given as ABERDONIAN (2) £40,000, CITY OF LONDON (2) £32,000, KOOLGA £30,000 and the tug ICH DIEN £1,600. The value of CITY LONDON (2) is rather surprising considering that her refit only some three years earlier had cost more than that !

In August 1929 the opportunity arose to acquire the London owned steamer SWIFT (1911) and as HARLAW (3) she arrived at Aberdeen on 28th October 1929. She had limited passenger accommodation, so took over the sailings in November from ABERDONIAN (2), when during the winter months passengers numbers were at a low level, with her running mate being the cargo-only KOOLGA. Some 15 months later a further passenger steamer, LAIRDSWOOD, was purchased from Glasgow owners. She could carry 140 saloon passengers as well as having superior steerage accommodation, had four hatches with steam cranes, and her two double-ended boilers burnt 25 tons of coal per day which gave her a speed of 14 knots. Built at Clydebank in 1906 as WOODCOCK (with her sister ship PARTRIDGE) and placed on sailings between Ardrossan and Belfast, both ships were taken up by the Admiralty on 15th November 1914 for service as fleet messengers. Fitted with three 12-pounder guns and renamed WOODNUT (to prevent confusion with another vessel of the same name), she sailed from Queens Dock, Glasgow on 8th December 1914 bound for Queenstown, southern Ireland, and thence to the Mediterranean. However, having arrived at Queenstown on 11th December (where she found her sister ship there also), defects in the structural changes made whilst fitting out as a warship came to light, and she was forced to abort her voyage south, She sailed from Queenstown for Glasgow on 12th January 1915 and returned to Yorkhill Basin, Glasgow for the necessary work to be carried out. After some weeks in dock, she eventually arrived in the Mediterranean. She was indeed to have "a long war" and saw many ports from Marseilles, Malta, Mudros and Constantinople during this time. It was not until 2nd August 1919 that she sailed from Malta with passengers and mails for Devonport. She arrived there on 11th August, and after being de-stored was de-commissioned on 23rd August 1919. However, she was not returned to her owners until 31st May 1920,

HARLAW (3) at anchor in the River Thames – note that World War 2 liferafts are still fitted.

(Aberdeen Maritime Museum)

LOCHNAGAR off Aberdeen, probably in 1931.

(Aberdeen Maritime Museum)

44

having first been refitted at Milford Haven and reverting to her name WOODCOCK. She was renamed LAIRDSWOOD in 1929 and sailed latterly between Glasgow and Dublin. The Company took her over at Ardrossan on 30th October 1930 and sailed her round to Aberdeen for refurbishing. She took up the sailings from 4th June 1931 renamed LOCHNAGAR.

CITY OF LONDON (2) was finally withdrawn from service after her arrival at Aberdeen on 21st November 1930. In February 1931 the 60 year-old iron steamer was sold to David MacBrayne Ltd. of Glasgow, sailing from Aberdeen for the last time on 3rd March bound for Ardrossan, where she was renamed LOCHBROOM. She sailed for a further six years on the west coast of Scotland for her new owners, until finally going to the breakers at Port Glasgow in July 1937.

Between 1931 and 1939 there were three passenger steamers and one cargo-only steamer available, although rarely were they all in service at any one time. A regular twice-weekly service to London was provided, with supplementary sailings as required, as passenger berths (during the summer months at least) once more became popular with tourists. The steamers were always kept in a smart condition with their hulls being painted black, boot-topping being red, and upperworks a wood-grained brown. The boats were painted brown and the ventilators buff to match the funnel colour. Passenger fares in the 1930s were very competitive for the journey to London and during the summer months the steamers attracted a large number of tourists. Two-berthed deck cabins and cabins-de-luxe were now also advertised in addition to four-berthed, and ICH DIEN now carried passengers to and from Westminster Pier in connection with the arrival and departures of the steamers.

THE END OF PASSENGER SAILINGS

War once again broke out on 3rd September 1939 and London passenger sailings were suspended after the arrival at Aberdeen of ABERDONIAN (2) on 1st September and LOCHNAGAR on 4th September, when both ships were laid-up. In February 1940 ABERDONIAN (2) was hired by the Admiralty as a depot ship for coastal forces, being first stationed at Fort William and later Dartmouth - she was in fact never to see Aberdeen Pier Heads again. LOCHNAGAR was hired at short notice by the Admiralty in April 1940 and sent in haste first to Scapa Flow, and then onwards to Norway to help evacuate the retreating Allied forces from Molde, Alesund and Andalsnes. She was employed from May 1940 in ferrying supplies to Iceland, and whilst so doing was involved in a collision at Reykjavik on 4th November 1941, as a result of which she received minor damage. On 10th November 1941, however, an explosion occurred resulting in a fire causing yet more damage and it was not until 21st December that she returned to Aberdeen. Worse was to come in the following year- on 26th December 1942, when on passage from Iceland to Aberdeen, she had an engine breakdown when in position 59.48N 09.18W (north of the island of St Kilda). She was taken in tow by a Royal Navy warship but unfortunately the tow parted the next day. However, she was able to proceed on her own at 4 knots and by the 28th had increased her speed to 8 knots by which time she was north of Cape Wrath and eventually arrived at Aberdeen some days later. After repairs costing £6,476 she resumed service again on 25th March 1942. Released from the Iceland sailings in January 1945, she was first employed sailing between Aberdeen and Lerwick from January until March 1945, and subsequently employed on other Government coastal sailings until early 1946.

KOOLGA and HARLAW (3) maintained the London sailings but a proposal was made in February 1940 that they be sold. This idea was rejected and sailings by these two vessels continued as wartime circumstances allowed. On 15th October 1940 all coastal and short-sea vessels came under the direction of the Ministry of Shipping, so at times from July 1944 KOOLGA and HARLAW (3) were taken off their normal route and operated from other ports, such as Dundee and Leith, to London. HARLAW (3) was attacked by German aircraft on 15th March 1941, when off Aberdeen, and 16th June 1941 when some 10 miles off Stonehaven, but only received relatively minor damage on both occasions. KOOLGA was not so fortunate when she was attacked on 2nd August 1941 whilst off Yarmouth, and the damage she suffered resulted in her being in dock at Yarmouth for two months. She was slightly damaged in another attack on 10th January 1942 when steaming between the Bell Rock and Arbroath. In August 1942 the tug ICH DIEN was sold for £1,500 to London owners, after serving the Company for 67 years. She remained afloat on the Thames until broken up in 1953.

Consideration was given in October 1943 as to whether the Company should become part of London Scottish Lines, a proposed organisation to be set up by Scottish coastal companies to merge sailings between Scotland and London. In July 1944 the proposition was declined as not being in the best interests of the Company. The same decision was also made by the Dundee, Perth & London Shipping Company, the Aberdeen, and the Newcastle & Hull Shipping Company.

With peace in Europe now seeming probable in the not so distant future, in May 1945 an approach to the Company was made by the Coast Lines group of Liverpool as to the possibility buying out the Company. A firm offer was received in June 1945 from the Tyne-Tees Steam Shipping Company Ltd. of Newcastle (a company within the Coast Lines group) to take the Company over, and this offer was accepted. It was all part of a move to rationalise coastal shipping in the light of the drift of passenger and cargo traffic from the sea to road and rail and the consequence loss of revenue.

LOCHNAGAR as she appeared during World War 2.

(National Maritime Museum)

The Company had already decided that passenger sailings would not be resumed when peace came because of the changed trading conditions, and the fact that the transportation of livestock by sea was no longer acceptable, further reducing the potential revenue of the Company. The age and condition of their three passenger steamers anyway was such that to re-introduce them into service would be expensive, so steps were put in hand to sell them by Coast Lines.

The transfer of control to the Tyne-Tees Steam Shipping Company Ltd. came about in November 1945, with the Company then becoming Coast Lines group agents at the same time. The new managers found that they had taken over an old and uneconomical fleet of four steamers, all heavily worked during the war, and all requiring extensive refurbishment. They proposed placing an order (when Government restrictions allowed) for two new motor ships capable of carrying 12 passengers each. On 2nd March 1946 all coastal and short sea shipping was derequisitioned by the Ministry of War Transport and the Company then had to grapple with peace time conditions again.

ABERDONIAN (2) had been de-stored at Devonport in March 1945, and returned to her owners at Plymouth on 3rd April. However, she remained laid-up at Plymouth until December 1945 when she was moved to Southampton for refurbishment prior to her sale. Whilst this work (at Government expense) was still under way, a provisional offer of £38,000 was made for her. However, bringing her up to standard took so long that by the time she was ready for transfer in September 1946 the price had dropped to £35,700. She was eventually handed over to her new owners at Southampton on 4th December 1946. Renamed TAISHAN PEAK, she sailed round to Liverpool and loaded for Hong Kong. Her time in the Far East was short, as she was badly damaged in a typhoon in July 1948 and finally went to the breakers yard in 1950.

LOCHNAGAR had been released from Government service on 26th February 1946, and whilst the Company waited to hear whether the Government proposed bringing her back to commercial standards again, she was laid-up at Aberdeen - she did in fact never again sail for the Company, the 40-year old vessel being sold in August 1946 before any major work was carried out on her. She sailed, renamed RENA, for the Tyne on 8th October 1946 to be converted to burn oil fuel, and then gave her new owners a further six years of service in the Mediterranean before going to the breakers.

HARLAW (3) and KOOLGA continued to maintain the sailings to London, now with an intermediate call at Newcastle (the Aberdeen, Newcastle & Hull Steam Company Ltd. having abandoned their sailings to the Tyne), but in the light of the low amount of traffic offering, and movement of livestock a thing of the past, it was only seen as an interim arrangement.

HARLAW (3) made her final voyage for the Company when she arrived at Aberdeen from London on 6th October 1946, having being sold for £33,500. She sailed to Newcastle on 24th October 1946, where she was handed over to her Chinese owners, and left the Tyne as MIN CHIH in December 1946, loaded coal at Barry, South Wales and sailed for Shanghai via Colombo on 16th January 1947. She was to make the newspaper headlines on at least three occasions after that, being taken over by her Chinese Nationalist crew in August 1953 and sailed to Taiwan. Later released, she was involved in a collision in January 1955 but made port, and in March 1955 was intercepted by a Chinese Nationalist warship but subsequently released, before finally arriving at the breakers at Hong Kong in August 1963.

KOOLGA made her final voyage for the Company when she arrived at Aberdeen from London on 21st October 1946, then sailed for Barry, South Wales on the 24th, where she arrived on 28th October 1946, having been sold for £30,000. She was there handed over to her Chinese owners, who renamed her MIN YUNG. It was not until 25th February 1947, however, that she sailed from Barry, but now under the Panamanian flag and named BEATRIZ. She was later sold to Swiss owners and traded in northern Europe waters until broken up in Germany in July 1953.

NEW OWNERS, NEW FUNNEL

As replacements for the ageing vessels, an order was placed on 27th September 1946 with the local yard of Hall, Russell & Company Ltd, for two twin-screw motor vessels, fitted to carry 12 passengers now that passenger traffic was at a very low level. Meantime, until delivery of the new ships, the Tyne-Tees Steam Shipping Company Ltd. allocated the small cargo-only motor vessel VALERIAN COAST (586/38) to the sailings, and she departed for the first time from Aberdeen on 24th October 1946. The operation of the service by just one small ship caused an outcry from shippers because of a lack of cargo capacity at times. During the stormier months of the year, a late arrival at Aberdeen caused additional problems. The vessel, having normally just a one-day turn round at Aberdeen, had to sail sometimes before loading was completed, excluding cargo already on the quayside, in order to maintain the weekly schedule. In early 1947 she had to be supplemented by the allocation from time to time of FRISIAN COAST (598/37) or OLIVIAN COAST (749/46), from the Tyne-Tees Steam Shipping Company fleet.

The first of the two new built passenger ships ordered from Hall Russell & Company Ltd, ABERDONIAN COAST, launched on 27th September 1946 and costing £178,072, made her maiden voyage from Aberdeen to London via Newcastle on 1st June 1947. Her yellow funnel now sported a wide green band and her hull was

VALERIAN COAST

painted white. FRISIAN COAST, the current vessel operating the sailings, departed for Liverpool on 28th May. Unfortunately, within three months faults developed on the masts, derricks and samson posts on ABERDONIAN COAST and she had to be withdrawn from service for the equipment to be strengthened, not coming back into service again until 16th December 1947. FRISIAN COAST was hurriedly recalled to take her place.

Meantime the second sister ship, CALEDONIAN COAST, was

ABERDONIAN COAST lying at Free Trade Wharf, River Thames.

(Graeme Somner collection)

launched on 1st October 1948, but unfortunately her delivery was delayed by her engine plate being dropped and damaged at the maker's works in Glasgow. This resulted in a delay of six weeks in the fitting of the engine whilst a new plate could be forged. In the light of the problems with the handling gear on her sister ship, the opportunity to modify it was taken, and the winch platform between Numbers 1 and 2 holds was removed. This latter modification was also carried out on ABERDONIAN COAST in June 1948. CALEDONIAN COAST made her maiden voyage on 21st April 1948, when she sailed from Aberdeen for Burntisland, on the Firth of Forth, for speed trials. She then proceeded onwards to Newcastle and London.

CALEDONIAN COAST entering Aberdeen Harbour   *(Graeme Somner collection)*

It was soon found that post-war labour conditions in the Port of London made it difficult to maintain a passenger schedule, and when a 15-day strike took place in that port at the end of June 1948, the Company decided to withdraw the passenger ships permanently. The sister ships were transferred to the ownership of the parent company, Coast Lines, at the beginning of July 1948, and then employed on the Liverpool-Dublin-South Coast-London sailings instead. The Company was invited by the Tyne-Tees Steam Shipping Company to then select two out of three vessels from their fleet for transfer to them. On offer were the cargo motor vessels HADRIAN COAST (692/42) at a book value of £44,600, VALERIAN COAST (586/38), book value £12,500, and OLIVIAN COAST (749/46), book value £91,000. The first two vessels were selected and transferred to the Company on 1st July 1948.

As a temporary measure, FRISIAN COAST arrived back again at Aberdeen on 2nd July to take up the sailings once more, the first being on 4th July. She was joined on 7th July by VALERIAN COAST (which was shortly afterwards more suitably renamed HEBRIDEAN COAST). In September 1948 HADRIAN COAST relieved FRISIAN COAST. Passenger sailings between Aberdeen and London were now a thing of the past.

By April 1949 there was insufficient traffic for two vessels so HEBRIDEAN COAST was time chartered to the Tyne-Tees Steam Shipping Company Ltd., and she was only to be seen in Aberdeen after that when relieving HADRIAN COAST for her annual overhaul. Eventually in February 1951 HEBRIDEAN COAST was transferred back to Tyne-Tees Steam Shipping Company Ltd. (book value now £12,800). Under group arrangements, any vessel not used in any one year by her nominated owner at least 50% of the time, was transferred to the member of the group with whom she had been employed.

From time to time conditions outside the Company's control, such as a late harvest resulting in bagged grain not coming forward for shipment, or a strike at the Aberdeen paper mills reducing the tonnage of paper available for shipment, caused trade to fluctuate. HADRIAN COAST broke down on 1st September 1954 whilst heading north and limped into Immingham, and it was not until 20th September that she was able to sail again. On 5th October 1954 a strike in the Port of London brought chaos to coastal sailings, and HADRIAN COAST had to sail north with whatever she had loaded. She then had to remain at Aberdeen until 5th November. Aberdeen Wharf on the Thames was very under-utilised now that only one vessel was calling there weekly, and despite efforts to find other vessels in other trades to fill the berth when HADRIAN COAST was not there, the Company had little success in finding such alternative traffic. In April 1956 Aberdeen Wharf passed into the control of others and the loading berth at London became Ratcliffe Cross Wharf.

FATEFUL TIMES

The Aberdeen to London sailings were maintained from 1948 onwards by HADRIAN COAST, relieved for a fortnight overhaul once a year until 1953 by HEBRIDEAN COAST. In 1954 the relief was undertaken by FRISIAN COAST, and in 1956 it was DURHAM COAST - she was in fact the very same HEBRIDEAN COAST with a new name! By April 1961, in a vain attempt to maintain viability, various other additional ports of call had been introduced. At Middlesbrough, Hull and Grimsby calls were made to pick up cargo on behalf of Tyne-Tees Steam Shipping Company destined for London. An additional call at Kirkcaldy (the Dundee, Perth & London Shipping Company had withdrawn their service in November 1957) was also introduced from November 1961, to load linoleum and other floor coverings on the way south.

52

HADRIAN COAST outward bound from London.

But the writing was on the wall. In June 1962 the linoleum trade at Kirkcaldy collapsed, and without this traffic, the sailings became completely unsustainable. HADRIAN COAST was chartered to the British Channel Islands Shipping Company Ltd. (part of the Coast Lines group) for a short time. A decision was then made to withdraw the London sailings and the last sailing from Aberdeen for London was made on 4th July, with the HADRIAN COAST finally returning to her berth at Waterloo Quay on 11th July 1962.

HADRIAN COAST was again chartered to the British Channel Island Shipping Company Ltd. to operate between London and the Channel Islands for a further period, but in February 1964 was transferred to Coast Lines. She was sold to Greek owners in 1967. On 17th February 1964 The Aberdeen Steam Navigation Company discontinued trading as a separate organisation within the Coast Lines group. Property and assets at London were transferred at book value to the Tyne-Tees Steam Shipping Company, whilst those at Aberdeen were transferred to The North of Scotland, Orkney & Shetland Shipping Company, part of the Coast Lines group from 1961. The Coast Lines group itself was absorbed by the Peninsular & Oriental Steam Navigation Company in 1971. The only physical object still to be seen that has any connection with the Company is the office building itself at 87 Waterloo Quay - still in use to-day and occupied by several small companies. The reconstructed quay itself is now used by tankers and oil rig support vessels.

After 126 years the Company has ceased to exist and all cargo and passengers journeying from Aberdeen to London now travelled by air, rail or road - sea travel, available for some 140 years since at least 1821, was no longer an option. At Waterloo Quay where there used to be the clatter of steam cranes working, and the noise of hoofs and feet crossing gangways, there is now silence. Dockers no longer handle anything from crates of whisky, bags of grain, boxes of fish and rolls of paper to "tatties, beasties and folk, and the constant din o' their toiling is heard nae mair".

FLEET LIST.

Notes

1. The notation (1), (2), (3), etc after a ship's name indicates the first, second etc ship of that name in the fleet.
2. The dates following the name are those of entry and leaving the ownership of The Aberdeen Steam Navigation Company Ltd.
3. All powered vessels were constructed of steel and were screw propelled unless otherwise stated.
4. The Official Number allocated to the vessel is shown after the letters "O.N.".
5. Tonnages of sailing vessels are "registered" (reg.), with those of powered vessels being gross - "g.", and net - "n.".
6. Dimensions of all vessels are registered length x beam x depth to the nearest foot for sailing vessels, and in feet and tenths of a foot for powered vessels.
7. Details of ships's engines show (for steamers) whether simple, compound or triple expansion, and (for motor vessels) the number of stroke cycles (SC) of the single acting engine (SA), and the number of cylinders (cyl.)
8. Horse power is shown for steamers as "hp" - registered or nominal, and for motor vessels as "bhp" - brake horse power.
9. The date shown is that of launching (if known) and/or date of completion. Where the builder's yard number is known, this is shown in brackets after the builder's name.

A. Sailing Ships.

1. NIMROD   **1821-1836**   **Wooden smack**
141 reg.   75 x 21 x 13 feet
9.1817: Launched by Richard Bussell, Lyme Regis. *3.1818:* Completed for George Thompson, John Lumsden & Robert Catto, Aberdeen. *1821:* Transferred to Aberdeen & London Shipping Co. *10.1836:* Sold to Andrew & William Phillips, Aberdeen for £912, rig altered to hermaphrodite by A.Hall & Co., Aberdeen, name unchanged *6.1844:* Sold to John Webster & Alexander Eddie, Aberdeen, name unchanged. *19.12.1844:* Driven onto North Pier, Aberdeen in a gale and lost.

2. MANSFIELD   **1821-1837**   **Wooden smack**
len. *1821* - 146 reg.   72 x 26 x 12 feet
1802: Completed by William Good, Bridport. *1805:* Now registered at Aberdeen. *7.1821:* Lengthened by Nicol, Reid & Co., Aberdeen, owners now Aberdeen & London Shipping Co. *3.1837:* Sold to Gordon of Banff for £720, name unchanged. Wrecked - date unknown .

3. BON ACCORD   **1824-1840**   **Wooden brigantine**
155 reg.   74 x 21 x 13 feet
1.1824: Launched by Richard Bussell, Lyme Regis for Aberdeen & London Shipping Co. *4.1824:* Completed. *11.1836:* Transferred to The Aberdeen Steam Navigation Co. *7.1840:* Sold to James Shrimps, Dundee, name unchanged. *9.1842:* Foundered off Holland.

4. BETSY   **1826-1833**   **Wooden hermaphrodite**
123 reg.   74 x 20 x 12 feet
5.1826: Completed by William Rennie, Aberdeen for Aberdeen & London Shipping Co. *5.1833:* Sold to Swainston & Cram, Liverpool, name unchanged. *11.1836:* Sold to P.M. Lamb & S. Green of Youghal, name unchanged. *8.1839:* Sold to T. Williams, King's Lynn, name unchanged. *1.1840:* Sold to William Shipp, King's Lynn, name unchanged. *2.1842:* Wrecked - details unknown.

5. DUKE OF GORDON   **1827-1837**   **Wooden smack**
150 reg.   75 x 21 x 13 feet
1.1827: Completed by Nicol, Reid & Co., Aberdeen for Aberdeen & London Shipping Co. *11.1836:* Transferred to Aberdeen Steam Navigation Co. *3.1837:* Sold to George Leslie, Aberdeen and re-rigged as a brigantine by Alexander Hall & Co., Aberdeen, name unchanged. *9.1839:* Sold to Walter Gray & Co., Glasgow, name unchanged. *5.1842:* Sold to William Waddell, Glasgow, name unchanged. *11.1852:* Broken up at Elsinore, Denmark.

6. TRUE BLUE   **1827-1836**   **Wooden hermaphrodite**
105 reg.   66 x 26 x 11 feet
1.1827: Completed by Robert & Peter Mathieson, Aberdeen for Aberdeen & London Shipping Co. *12.1836:* Sold to Neil Smith & Co., Aberdeen, name unchanged. *4.1837:* Sold to John Ogilvey, Aberdeen, name unchanged. *6.1840:* Sold to Robert Spring, Aberdeen, name unchanged. *7.1843:* Sold to William Leask, Aberdeen, name unchanged. *4.1844:* Sold to John Ballintine, Lyme Regis, name unchanged. *14.9.1848:* Condemned and sold at Gothenburg for breaking up.

7. SUPERIOR **1839-1852** **Wooden smack/brigantine**
O.N.6883 144 reg. 75 x 21 x 13 feet
1814: Completed by Richard Bussell, Lyme Regis. *4.1816:* Known to have been owned by Aberdeen & Hull Shipping Co. *4.1837:* Re-rigged as a brigantine by A.Hall & Co., Aberdeen. *7.1839:* Purchased by Aberdeen Steam Navigation Co., name unchanged. *10.1852:* Sold to Andrew Anderson, Aberdeen, re-rigged as a brig, name unchanged. *2.1855:* Sold to Aberdeen Whale Fishing Co., Aberdeen, name unchanged. *7.1859:* Sold to Godfrey McTaggart, Arbroath, name unchanged. *10.1866:* Owner now Donald M. McTaggart, Aberdeen. *3.1870:* Sold to Thomas Darling, jnr., Aberdeen, name unchanged. *2.1872:* Sold to George Campbell, Aberdeen, name unchanged. *7.1873:* Sold to Alexander Wishart & Hugh Geddes (of Newcastle), Aberdeen, name unchanged. *7.1881:* Owners now James E. Lawson & Crawford Noble, jnr. *2.1882:* Sold to Crawford Noble, jnr. & James S. Noble, Aberdeen, name unchanged. *5.1883:* Sold to James E. Lawie, Aberdeen, name unchanged. *12.1884:* Sold to W. Geddes, Aberdeen, name unchanged. *3.1885:* Reduced to a hulk.

8. THETIS **1839-1840** **Wooden smack**
94 reg. 63 x 19 x 11 feet
11.1826: Completed by William Rennie, Aberdeen for Aberdeen & Hull Shipping Co., Aberdeen. *7.1839:* Purchased by Aberdeen Steam Navigation Co., name unchanged. *2.1840:* Sold to Thomas Ostrich, Hull and re-rigged as a schooner, name unchanged. *3.8.1844:* Foundered in Oxwick Bay, west of the Mumbles, South Wales, while on passage from Cardiff to Rotterdam with a cargo of coal.

9. FLORENCE **1839-1849** **Wooden smack**
O.N.6862 128 reg. 76 x 19 x 11 feet
10.1831: Completed by William Rennie, Aberdeen for Aberdeen & Hull Shipping Co., Aberdeen, original length 66 feet, 94 reg. *7.1839:* Purchased by Aberdeen Steam Navigation Co., name unchanged. *11.1839:* Lengthened 10 feet by Alexander Hall & Co., Aberdeen. *7.1849:* Sold to John Stewart & Joseph Russell, Aberdeen, name unchanged. *7.1851:* Sold to Andrew Crane, Aberdeen, re-rigged as a schooner, name unchanged. *2.1866:* Sold to F.D. Lambert, London, name unchanged. *10.1875:* Sold to J.J. Saffrey, London, name unchanged. *1.1876:* Sold to Dutch owners - no further record.

10. PARAGON **1842-1853** **Wooden schooner**
O.N.812 153 reg. 100 x 21 x 12 feet
11.1842: Completed by Duthie & Co., Aberdeen for Aberdeen Steam Navigation Co. *5.1853:* Sold to William Lawson (of Whitstable) Faversham, name unchanged. *21.2.1862:* Destroyed by fire in Plymouth Sound while bound for London.

11. ABERDONIAN (1) **1844-1853** **Wooden schooner**
O.N.5337 149 reg. 96 x 20 x 12 feet
5.1840: Completed by Alexander Hall & Co., Aberdeen for Nicol & Munro, Aberdeen. *1.1844:* Purchased by Aberdeen Steam Navigation Co., name unchanged. *6.1853:* Sold to George & James Leslie, Aberdeen, name unchanged. *2.1871:* Sold to Daniel Mearns, Aberdeen, name unchanged. *6.1883:* Sold to J. Archibald, Aberdeen, name unchanged. *3.1888:* Broken up.

12. LONDON **1844-1850** **Wooden schooner**
143 reg. 96 x 20 x 12 feet
7.1840: Completed by Alexander Hall & Co., Aberdeen for Nicol & Munro, Aberdeen. *1.1844:* Purchased by Aberdeen Steam Navigation Co., name unchanged. *2.1850:* Lost.

13. WILLIAM HOGARTH **1844-1846** **Wooden schooner**
140 reg. 92 x 19 x 13 feet
5.1841: Completed by Bowman Vernon & Co., Aberdeen for Nicol & Munro, Aberdeen. *2.1844:* Purchased by Aberdeen Steam Navigation Co., name unchanged. *10.1846:* Sold to Aberdeen, Leith & Clyde Shipping Co., Aberdeen, name unchanged. *9.2.1852:* Sailed from Aberdeen for Lerwick and not heard of again - a force 11 gale was blowing in the area at the time.

14. GAZELLE **1846-1853** **Wooden schooner**
O.N.40185 175 reg. 101 x 20 x 13 feet
5.1846: Completed by Walter Hood & Co., Aberdeen for Aberdeen Steam Navigation Co. *8.1853:* Sold for £1,500 to Murdoch McKenzie, Melbourne, name unchanged. *1856:* Now registered at Auckland. *1860:* Lost in China Seas.

B. POWERED VESSELS.

1. QUEEN OF SCOTLAND	1827-1843	Wooden paddle
O.N.5347	430g 305n	149.1 x 26.5 x 18.0 feet
	len. 1843 - 593g 421n	166.3 x 26.3 x 16.4 feet

Engines (2) by builders, 150hp
16.4.1827: Launched by John Duffus & Co., Aberdeen for Aberdeen & London Steam Navigation Co. (John Duffus & Co., managers). *17.8.1827:* Registered. *1.1843:* Sold to Joseph Gee & Co., Hull, name unchanged. *8.1843:* Lengthened. *4.1860:* Sold to Thomas Hodson & others, Manchester, name and port of register unchanged. *10.1863:* Sold to C.M. Lofthouse & R. Glover, Hull, name unchanged. *1869:* Broken up.

2. DUKE OF WELLINGTON	1829-1850	Wooden paddle
	335n	154.0 x 27.8 x 18.7 feet

Engines (2) by builders, 181hp
4.1829: Completed by John Duffus & Co., Aberdeen for Aberdeen & London Steam Navigation Co. (John Duffus & Co., managers). *4.1850:* Broken up.

3. CITY OF ABERDEEN (1)	1835-1858	Wooden paddle
O.N.24742	877g 553n	165.5 x 28.5 x 19.5 feet
	Len. 11.1841 - 962g 663n	188.9

Simple side lever, 2-cyl. by Scott, Sinclair & Co., Greenock, 240hp
5.1835: Completed by John Scott & Sons, Greenock for Aberdeen & London Steam Navigation Co. (John Duffus & Co., managers). *11.1841:* Lengthened by Alexander Duthie & Co., Aberdeen. *20.3.1855:* Requisitioned for service as a transport in the Crimea and sailed from Devonport for Constantinople. *16.6.1855:* Returned from the Black Sea. *1.1858:* Sold to James & Peter Denny, Dumbarton, name and port of register unchanged, for £4,000 as part payment for DUKE OF ROTHESAY. *5.1859:* Sold to N.S. Begbie, London, name unchanged. *9.1859:* Arrived at Liverpool from Genoa and Malaga and laid-up. *6.1860:* Sold to Sicilian Government, renamed ROSALINO PILO, and incorporated into Italian Navy as a transport - no further record.

CITY OF ABERDEEN (1)   *(University of Glasgow)*

4. DUCHESS OF SUTHERLAND	1838-1847	Wooden paddle
	575g 329n	151.0 x 24.8 x 17.0 feet
	Len. 4.1841 - 718g 462n	181.0

Engines (2)
3.1836: Completed by Wood & Miles, Dumbarton for Moray Firth & London Steam Packet Co., Inverness.   *4.1838:* Purchased by Aberdeen Steam Navigation Co., name unchanged. *4.1841:* Lengthened by Alexander Duthie & Co., Aberdeen. *6.1846:* Laid-up at Aberdeen. *9.1846:* Advertised for sale. *9.1847:* Sold to Robert Napier, Glasgow, name unchanged, as part payment for two new ships, DUKE OF SUTHERLAND and EARL OF ABERDEEN. *1.1851:* Broken up at Glasgow.

5. CITY OF LONDON (1)   **1844-1871**   **Iron paddle/screw**
O.N.26349   1067g 723n   221.5 x 24.3 x 19.2 feet
Direct acting, 2-cyl. by builders, 420hp; fitted 6.1869, oscillating, 2-cyl., engine
by Bolton & Co., Birmingham 250hp
7.1844: Completed by R. Napier & Sons, Glasgow (4) for Aberdeen Steam Navigation Co.
2.2.1854: Requisitioned for service in connection with Crimean War. *30.11.1855:* Returned to
commercial service. *24.7.1866:* Broke shaft off Cromer, Norfolk while on passage from
Aberdeen to London. *16.8.1866:* Returned to service, her sailings meantime being operated
by the chartered OSSIAN (721/55) of London & Edinburgh Shipping Co., Leith. *6.1871:* Sold
to George Russell & Co., London, name unchanged. *1887:* Broken up.

6. NORTH STAR   **1845-1853**   **Wooden paddle**
O.N. 31745   453g 306n   161.0 x 25.3 x 13.7 feet
Engines (2)
4.1837: Completed by John Duffus & Co., Aberdeen for their own account (James Sims,
George Elsmie jnr, & William Reid, all merchants), trading as the North of Scotland Steam
Navigation Co. *10.1845:* Purchased by Aberdeen Steam Navigation Co., name unchanged.
6.1853: Sold to John Borrie & Thomas E. Boyd, Dundee, name unchanged. Engines
unshipped and vessel sailed to Australia. *5.1856:* Sold to Thomas Dickson & James
Lawrence, Melbourne, name unchanged. *1864:* Registered shows owners unknown. *1871:*
Deleted from Register.

7. DUKE OF SUTHERLAND   **1847-1853**   **Iron paddle**
    803g 515n   197.9 x 26.2 x 17.5 feet
No engine details available
3.1847: Completed by R. Napier & Sons, Glasgow (21) for Aberdeen Steam Navigation Co.
1.4.1853: Driven onto North Pier, Aberdeen whilst entering port during a heavy swell and
became a total loss - 16 lost.

8. EARL OF ABERDEEN   **1847-1863**   **Iron paddle**
O.N.6837   907g 505n   207.9 x 27.0 x 17.8 feet
2-cyl. by builders, 380hp
7.1847: Built by R. Napier & Sons, Glasgow (22) for Aberdeen Steam Navigation Co.
30.5.1855: Requisitioned in connection with the Crimean War and sailed from Portsmouth for
Constantinople. *9.2.1856:* Returned to commercial service. *4.1863:* With a need to spend
£10,000 on repairs and re-boilering, sold to General Steam Navigation Co., London for
£9,000. *1880:* Broken up.

9. ROYAL VICTORIA   **1855-1857**   **Wooden paddle**
O.N.335   ? g   354n   155.3 x 28.0 x 19.0 feet
    1840 - 656g 366n   165.6
220hp
4.1835: Completed by Robert Menzies & Son, Leith for London, Leith, Edinburgh & Glasgow
Shipping Co., Leith. *1840:* Lengthened. *3.1855:* Purchased by Aberdeen Steam Navigation
Co., name unchanged. *12.1857:* Broken up.

10. COMMODORE   **1855-1859**   **Wooden paddle**
O.N.23391   760g 358n   176.5 x 25.2 x 19.1 feet
2-cyl. 360hp
2.1838: Completed by John Wood, Port Glasgow for City of Glasgow Steam Packet Co. (for
Glasgow-Liverpool sailings). *1.1846:* Sold to Charles MacIver & Co., Liverpool, name
unchanged (for Liverpool-Southampton-Havre sailings). *3.1855:* Sold to Peter Denny,
Dumbarton, name and port of register unchanged. *3.1855:* Purchased by Aberdeen Steam
Navigation Co., name unchanged. *16.9.1859:* Wrecked at Fife Ness, Fife.

11. DUKE OF ROTHESAY   **1857-1859**   **Iron screw**
O.N.15790   578g 393n   187.8 x 2.28 x 15.4 feet
2-cyl. 180hp
13.2.1857: Launched by William Denny & Bros., Dumbarton (62) for Aberdeen Steam
Navigation Co. *3.1857:* Completed. *16.7.1859:* Sailed from Aberdeen for London and Cadiz,
where she sold was to the Spanish Government for £14,000 - no further record.

12. GAMBIA   **1861-1870**   **Iron screw**
O.N. 26622   517g 352n   191.9 x 26.2 x 14.3 feet
Engines (2), 80hp
7.1855: Completed at Port Glasgow for The African Steam Ship Co., London. *12.1859:* Sold
to John Stewart, Aberdeen, name unchanged. *11.1861:* Purchased by Aberdeen Steam
Navigation Co., name unchanged. *7.1.1870:* Foundered off Dudgeon Light Vessel while on
passage from London to Aberdeen, all passengers and crew saved.

12A. KANGAROO   **Iron screw**
O.N.16279   458g 312n   167.5 x 23.2 x 12.6 feet
Engines (2), 60hp
10.1853: Completed by Smith & Rodgers, Govan, Glasgow for Waterford Steam Ship Co.
(Malcolmson Bros., managers), Waterford.   *6.1858:* Sold to Alexander & David Dunn,
London, name unchanged.   *11.1859:* Owner now David Dunn (manager of the Northern
Steam Navigation Co.), Aberdeen, name unchanged.   *20.1.1862:* Put into Cairn Ryan, near
Stranraer, to shelter from a storm, while on passage from the Clyde to Bordeaux. *23.1.1862:*
Foundered in force 10 gale when 10 miles south of South Stack, Angelsey, with loss of 13 of
her 20 crew.

13. STANLEY   **1861-1864**   **Iron screw**
O.N. 27448   553g 376n   193.9 x 27.0 x 14.1 feet
Engines (2), 110hp
4.1859: Completed at West Hartlepool for James Jack, Liverpool. *1.1861:* Sold to John
Stewart, Aberdeen, name unchanged. *11.1861:* Acquired by Aberdeen Steam Navigation Co.,
name unchanged. *24.11.1864:* Wrecked on Spanish Battery Rocks at entrance to River Tyne
in force 10 gale, whilst inbound from Aberdeen with 30 crew and 30 passengers - 4 crew and
22 passengers lost.

14. CITY OF ABERDEEN (2)   **1865-1871**   **Iron screw**
O.N.53242   682g 440n   227.5 x 29.4 x 16.0 feet
2-cyl. 160hp, 11 knots
10.1865: Completed by R. Duncan & Co., Port Glasgow for the Company. *20.1.1871:* Stranded
at Portlethen, 7 miles south of Aberdeen, whilst in bound to Aberdeen, and became a total
loss - landfall made but insufficient action taken by mate to avoid stranding.

15. BAN-RIGH   **1870-1901**   **Iron screw**
O.N.60704   958g 576n   241.0 x 30.2 x 16.6 feet
Compound, 2-cyl. by builders, 275nhp; new triple, 3-cyl. fitted 1893, Hall,
Russell & Co., Aberdeen, 236nhp
3.3.1870: Launched by J. Elder & Co, Port Glasgow (112) for the Company.   *3.1870:*
Completed.   *10.1901:* Sold for breaking up but resold to R. de Paula. for employment by
Columbian Government.   *11.1901:* Vessel declared a pirate by Venezuelan Government with
a reward of $10,000 offered for her capture. *1.1902:* Now renamed LIBERTADOR.   *5.1902:*
Now renamed BOLIVAR.   *1904:* Now owned by Colombian Government, registered at
Cartagena, and renamed MARROQUIN. *1927:* Omitted from Lloyd's Register.

16. CITY OF LONDON (2)   **1871-1931**   **Iron screw**
O.N.65079   977g 565n   241.9 x 30.5 x 16.7 feet
Compound, 2-cyl. by builders, 275nhp
8.6.1871: Launched by J. Elder & Co., Port Glasgow (135) for the Company.   *6.1871:*
Completed.   *13.8.1879:* Sank in Barking Reach, River Thames after being run into by German
steamer VESTA (1030/79). *15.8.1879:* Raised and beached - later repaired. *2.1931:* Sold to
David MacBrayne Ltd., Glasgow and renamed LOCHBROOM (for summer service Glasgow-
Western Isles). *7.1937:* Broken up by Smith & Houston Ltd., Port Glasgow.

17. CITY OF ABERDEEN (3)   **1873-1906**   **Iron screw**
O.N.65094   972g 580n   240.8 x 30.1 x 16.6 feet
Compound, 2-cyl. by builders, 300nhp
3.1873: Completed by Cunliffe & Dunlop, Port Glasgow (87) for the Company. *10.1906:* Sold
to Limassol S.S.Co., Piraeus and renamed SALAMIS. *1915:* Sold to Nicolaou & Co., Piraeus,
name unchanged.   *1917:* Sold to D.F. Andreadis, Syra, name unchanged.   *24.2.1917:*
Torpedoed and sunk by German submarine UC 17 in Bay of Biscay while on passage from
Barry to Bordeaux with a cargo of coal.

18. HOGARTH (1)   **1876-1878**   **Iron screw**
O.N.70456   567g 355n   195.1 x 26.2 x 14.0 feet
Compound, 2-cyl. by builders, 150hp
9.1876: Completed by Cunliffe & Dunlop, Port Glasgow for the Company. *8.1878:* Sold to
London & South Western Railway Co., Southampton and renamed CALEDONIA. *19.2.1881:*
Struck Oyster Rock off St Helier, Jersey, while on passage from Southampton and sank.
2.4.1881: Sold to Gautier de Ste. Croix of St. Helier for £140, who recovered her boiler and
engine for scrap.

19. ICH DIEN   **1877-1942**   **Iron screw tug**
O.N.77438   87g 24n   94.8 x 17.1 x 8.7 feet
Compound, 2-cyl. by builders, 40hp
8.1877: Completed by Cunliffe & Dunlop, Port Glasgow (130) for the Company, for service as
tender/tug on the River Thames. *9.1942:* Sold to R.G. Odell Ltd., London, name unchanged.
9.1953: Broken up.

20. HARLAW (1)   1881-1888   Iron screw
O.N.84354   450g   267n   165.1 x 24.5 x 11.8 feet
Compound, 2-cyl. by builders, 71nhp
10.1881: Completed by Cunliffe & Dunlop, Port Glasgow (157) for the Company. *4.1888:* Sold to Halifax & Newfoundland S.S.Co. Ltd., (Pickford & Black, managers), Windsor, N.S., name unchanged. *7.4.1911:* Lost in ice in the Gulf of St. Lawrence, Canada, whilst on a seal hunt.

21. OITHONA   1887-1891   Steel screw
O.N.88875   701g   318n   205.2 x 27.5 x 15.2 feet
Triple, 3-cyl. by builders, 150nhp
21.9.1887: Launched by Hall, Russell & Co., Aberdeen (245) for the Company. *10.1887:* Completed. *9.1891:* Sold to Imperial Russian Navy for service as a despatch vessel. *2.1892:* Re-built by R. Craggs & Sons Ltd., Middlesbrough (under Yard No.102), registered at St. Petersburg, and renamed YACOUT (sometimes spelt YAKUT or IAKUT). *1.1921:* Arrived at Bizerta, Tunisia with the Russian Wrangell Squadron. *4.1923:* Sold to Emanuele Chetcuti, Valletta, Malta, issued with new Official Number 152048, and renamed G M LA VALLETTE. *4.1926:* Sold to A. Scamama-Lagardere, Tunis, name unchanged. *1934:* Sold to D. Papoulias & K. Tsesmelis, Spetsai and renamed IONION. *1937:* Sold to Guiseppe Riccardi, Genoa and believed broken up at Savona. (Still in register until 1947).

22. HOGARTH (2)   1893-1918   Steel screw
O.N.99647   1226g   645n   252.8 x 32.7 x 17.6 feet
Triple, 3-cyl. by builders, 345nhp
1.1893: Completed by Hall, Russell & Co., Aberdeen (275) for the Company. *22.11.1905:* Ran down fishing vessel POMEGRANATE off Lowestoft, seven lives lost. *7.6.1918:* Torpedoed and sunk by German submarine UB 107 off Longstone Light, Farne Islands, whilst on passage from London to Aberdeen with a general cargo. One survivor was picked up after nearly two days on a raft and landed in the Tyne, but 26 including the Master were lost.

23. HARLAW (2)   1899-1910   Steel screw
O.N.91315   821g   449n   220.5 x 29.1 x 13.7 feet
Triple, 3-cyl. by builders, 163nhp
7.1888: Built by Earle's Shipbuilding & Engineering Co. Ltd., Hull (310) for Yorkshire Coal & Steamship Co. Ltd., Goole as GOTHA. *12.1895:* Sold to Goole Steam Shipping Co. Ltd., Goole, name unchanged. *5.1899:* Purchased by Aberdeen Steam Navigation Co. *25.8.1899:* Ran ashore at Ness of Quoys, Caithness while on passage in ballast from Aberdeen to Lerwick. *29.8.1899:* Damaged sealed and flooded engine room pumped out, and then beached off Scrabster. *2.9.1899:* Sailed for Aberdeen for repairs to be carried out. *12.1910:* Sold to Patriotic S.S. Co. Ltd., London, name unchanged. *12.1912:* Sold to J. Constant, London, name unchanged. *8.1915:* Seized by Italian authorities and transferred to Italian State Railways, Palermo, name unchanged. *31.1.1918:* Sunk by gunfire of German submarine UB 48 when 30 miles north-west of Corsica.

24. ABERDONIAN (2)   1909-1946   Steel screw
O.N.127164   1648g   747n   264.3 x 36.2 x 18.3 feet
Triple, 3-cyl. by builders, 294nhp
5.1909: Completed by D & W. Henderson & Co. Ltd., Glasgow (466) for the Company. *1915:* Hired as a hospital ship for service in Mediterranean and English Channel. *4.1917:* Because of attacks on fully marked hospital ships became classed as an ambulance transport. *9.1919:* Resumed sailings. *2.1940:* Hired by the Admiralty as a depot ship for coastal forces, stationed at Fort William and later Dartmouth. *3.1945:* De-stored at Devonport and returned to owners and laid-up at Plymouth. *1.1946:* Drydocked at Southampton. *10.1946:* Sold to Peak Shipping Co. Ltd. (Lambert Bros. Ltd., managers), Hong Kong, name and port of register unchanged. *12.1946:* Renamed TAISHAN PEAK, port of register unchanged. *1.1947:* Sailed from Liverpool. *25.2.1947:* Arrived at Hong Kong, and port of register subsequently changed to that port. *2.1948:* Sold to Shahi S.S. Co. (Wallem & Co., managers), Panama and renamed PARVIZ. *7.1948:* Damaged in typhoon whilst lying at Hong Kong. *12.1949:* Sold for breaking up. *2.1950:* Broken up by Yusufally Akberali at Bombay.

25. KOOLGA   1918-1946   Steel screw
O.N.129384   1110g   564n   232.1 x 33.9 x 14.9 feet
Triple, 3-cyl. by builders, 188hp
10.3.1910: Launched by Caledon Shipbuilding & Engineering Co. Ltd., Dundee (213) for Thomas Cowan, Leith. *4.1910:* Completed. *12.1918:* Purchased by the Company, name unchanged. *2.8.1941:* Damaged in air attack off Smith's Knoll, Norfolk. *10.1946:* Sold to Min Kiang Steam Ship Co., Shanghai and renamed MIN YUNG. *11.1946:* Laid-up Barry, South Wales. *2.1947:* Sold to Cia. Maritima Sphika S. A., Panama and renamed BEATRIZ. *5.1947:* Sold to Kustenschiffart A. G. (Seetrans Schiffsagentur Lange & Co., managers), Basle and renamed GALLUS. *7.1953:* Arrived at Hamburg and later broken up.

S. S. "Hogarth."   Torpedoed in the North Sea on 8th June, 1918.

The Aberdeen Steam Navigation Company's fine Passenger Steamers sailing between London and Aberdeen every Wednesday and Saturday.

(Aberdeen Maritime Museum)

HOGARTH (2)

26. HARLAW (3)   1929-1946   Steel screw
O.N.132632   1141g 466n   244.8 x 34.6 x 14.2 feet
Triple, 3-cyl. by builders, 337nhp
26.8.1911: Launched by Ramage & Ferguson Ltd., Leith (226) for General Steam Navigation
Co. Ltd., London as SWIFT for employment on London-Leith sailings. *11.1911:* Completed.
8.1914: Hired by the Admiralty for service as a flotilla supply ship. *2.1915:* Renamed DEAN
SWIFT. *8.1915:* Returned to commercial service and employed on Rotterdam and Bordeaux
sailings. *3.1919:* Reverted to original name of SWIFT.   *8.1929:* Purchased by the Company
and renamed HARLAW. *11.11.1940:* Damaged in aircraft attack off Aberdeen. *10.1946:* Sold
to Min Kiang S.S.Co. Ltd., Shanghai and renamed MIN CHIH. *16.1.1947:* Sailed from Barry
for Shanghai via Colombo. *18.3.1947:* Arrived at Hong Kong. *1947:* Sold to Hai Ying
Steamship Co. Ltd., Shanghai and renamed HAI YANG. *1949:* Sold to Pacific Union S.S. Co.,
Panama and renamed CHEPO.   *1950:* Sold to Far Eastern & Panama Transport Corp.
(Wheelock, Marden & Co. Ltd., managers), Panama and renamed HOLLINA. *1950:* Sold to
Colon Shipping Co. S. A., Panama, name unchanged. *18.8.1953:* Sailed from Hong Kong but
whilst at sea seized by her pro-Nationalist crew. *23.8.1953:* Arrived at Kaohsiung, Taiwan
where cargo landed and looted. *16.9.1953:* Released and restored to owners. *3.11.1953:*
Sailed from Kaohsiung for Hong Kong. *1954:* Sold to Compania Maritima Oriental S. A.,
Panama and renamed EL BRENON.   *30.1.1955:* In collision 400 miles west of Sasebo with
British steamer BRIGHTON (4630/43), while on passage from Miike to Hong Kong, but
reached port safely. *3.1955:* Intercepted at sea by Nationalist Government warship but
released. *6.1959:* Sold to Victory S.S. Co., Panama and renamed TRIUMPH. *28.8.1963:*
Arrived at Hong Kong for breaking up.

27. LOCHNAGAR   1930-1946   Steel screw
O.N.121346   1619g 688n   270.4 x 36.1 x 16.6 feet
Triple, 3-cyl. by builders, 460nhp
10.4.1906: Launched by John Brown & Co. Ltd., Clydebank (372) for G. & J. Burns Ltd.,
Glasgow as WOODCOCK for Ardrossan-Belfast sailings. *6.1906:* Completed.   *15.11.1914:*
Hired by the Admiralty as an armed boarding ship and fleet messenger for service in the
Mediterranean and Aegean Seas, being renamed WOODNUT. *23.8.1919:* Decommissioned.
31.5.1920: Returned to owners after refit at Milford Haven and reverted to WOODCOCK.
6.1922: Owners amalgamated with Laird Line Ltd., Glasgow to form Burns and Laird Lines
Ltd. *5.1928:* To rationalise names within the fleet, renamed LAIRDSWOOD.   *10.1930:*
Purchased by the Company. *4.6.1931:* Entered service as LOCHNAGAR. *9.1939:* Laid-up at
Aberdeen. *4.1940:* Hired by the Admiralty to assist in evacuation of Allied Forces from
Norway. *5.1940:* On sailings between Aberdeen and Lerwick. *10.1941:* On sailings to Iceland.
1.1945: Operated between Aberdeen and Lerwick for two months, and then laid up at
Aberdeen. *8.1946:* Sold to Rena Cia. de Navegacion S. A., Panama and renamed RENA.
8.10.1946: Sailed from Aberdeen for the Tyne for conversion to oil fuel. *1951:* Renamed
BLUESTAR. *1952:* Broken up.

LOCHNAGAR – note canvas dodgers have now been fitted on the main and promenade decks
for the comfort of passengers.   *(Ballast Trust)*

28. ABERDONIAN COAST   **1947-1948**   **Steel twin-screw**
O.N.182013   1258g 637n   265.0 x 40.2 x 12.5 feet
Oil engines (2), each 2SCSA, 4-cyl. by British Polar Engines Ltd., Glasgow,
2560bhp, 14 kts
27.9.1946: Launched by Hall, Russell & Co. Ltd., Aberdeen (800) for The Aberdeen Steam
Navigation Co. Ltd. *5.1947:* Completed. *7.1948:* Transferred to Coast Lines Ltd., Liverpool,
name unchanged (for Liverpool-Dublin-South Coast-London sailings). *11.1948:* Renamed
HIBERNIAN COAST. *11.1968:* Sold to Alomar Mechanical Engineering Co., Kuwait and
renamed PORT SAID COAST. *1970:* Sold to Kuwait Coast Line Co., Kuwait, name unchanged.
5.1974: Broken up at Murcia, Spain.

29. CALEDONIAN COAST   **1948-1948**   **Steel twin-screw**
O.N.182018   1265g 637n   265.0 x 40.2 x 12.5 feet
Oil engines (2), each 2SCSA, 4-cyl. by British Polar Engines Ltd., Glasgow,
2560bhp, 14 kts
30.9.1947: Launched by Hall, Russell & Co. Ltd., Aberdeen (803) for The Aberdeen Steam
Navigation Co. Ltd. *4.1948:* Completed. *7.1948:* Transferred to Coast Lines Ltd., Liverpool (for
Liverpool-Dublin-South Coast-London sailings). *4.1967:* On long term charter to T & J.
Brocklebank Ltd., Liverpool (for service between Liverpool and Mediterranean), being
renamed MAKALLA. *11.1968:* Sold to Alomar Mechanical Engineering Co., Kuwait and
renamed AHMADI COAST. *1970:* Sold to Kuwait Coast Line Co., Kuwait, name unchanged.
8.4.1974: Arrived at Carthagena, Spain for breaking up.

CALEDONIAN COAST with Coast Lines funnel markings.   *(Graeme Somner collection)*

30. VALERIAN COAST/   **1946-1953**   **Steel screw**
     HEBRIDEAN COAST
O.N.165759   586g 276n   189.6 x 31.6 x 10.9 feet
Oil engine, 4SCSA, 6-cyl. by Humboldt-Deutzmoteron A.G., Koln-Deutz, 825bhp, 10 kts; new
engine fitted *2.1961* by same makers
2.1938: Built by N.V. Scheepswerf "Gideon" Voorhen J. Koster Hzn., Groningen (158) for
Tyne-Tees Steam Shipping Co. Ltd., Newcastle as SANDHILL. *6.1946:* On the company being
taken over by Coast Lines Ltd., renamed VALERIAN COAST. *10.1946:* Allocated to The
Aberdeen Steam Navigation Co. Ltd. for six months until new vessel available. *7.1948:*
Transferred to The Aberdeen Steam Navigation Co. Ltd. and renamed HEBRIDEAN COAST.
4.1949: Chartered to Tyne-Tees Steam Shipping Co. Ltd. *2.1951:* Transferred to Tyne-Tees
Steam Shipping Co. Ltd., name unchanged. *6.1953:* Transferred to Belfast S.S. Co. Ltd.,
Belfast and renamed ULSTER CHIEFTAIN. *2.1956:* Transferred to Tyne-Tees Steam Shipping
Co. Ltd., Newcastle and renamed DURHAM COAST. *2.1960:* Transferred to British & Irish
Steam Packet Co. Ltd., Dublin and renamed WICKLOW. *1970:* Sold to Sistillac Shipping Co.
Ltd., Famagusta and renamed SINERGASIA. *1973:* Sold to Agios Sostis Maritime Co. Ltd.,
Famagusta and renamed SONIA. *1974:* Sold to Fortitude Maritime Co., Greek flag, and
renamed MARGARITA P. *1976:* Sold to Cia. de Nav. Scotia, S. A., Panama, name unchanged.
9.5.1979: Arrived at Baia, Italy and laid-up. *1980:* Broken up at Baia by Cantiere Navale
Nettuno.

31. HADRIAN COAST   **1948-1964**   **Steel screw**
O.N.168807   692g 247n   201.3 x 33.2 x 11.1 feet
Oil engine, 2SCSA, 7-cyl. by British Auxiliaries Ltd., Glasgow, 11 kts
12.7.1941: Launched by Ardrossan Dockyard Co. Ltd., Ardrossan (385), ordered by Coast
Lines Ltd., Liverpool as a refrigerated coaster, and completed for the Ministry of War
Transport as EMPIRE ATOLL, being managed by Coast Lines Ltd., Liverpool. *1.1942:*
Completed. *12.1946:* Sold to Tyne-Tees Steam Shipping Co. Ltd., Newcastle, refrigeration
machinery removed, and renamed HADRIAN COAST. *9.1948:* Transferred to The Aberdeen
Steam Navigation Co. Ltd., name unchanged. *2.1964:* Transferred to Coast Lines Ltd.,
Liverpool, name unchanged. *9.1967:* Sold to E. Daviou, D. Agoudimos & A. Klissiaunis,
Piraeus and renamed ELDA. *10.1.1970:* Driven ashore in a storm 2 miles east of Mehdiya,
Morocco, while on passage from Ravenna, Italy, to Kenitra, Morocco, and became a total
loss.

87 Waterloo Quay – the office building, put up in 1841, and still standing today.

64

ABERDONIAN (2) off Woolwich, River Thames on 4th July 1934.   *(Snook collection)*

HEBRIDEAN COAST   *(W.S.P.L.)*

INDEX OF SHIPS' NAMES

Ship's names in CAPITALS are those carried when the vessel was owned by The Aberdeen Steam Navigation Company Ltd. Those names in lower case are those when owned by other companies.

Ship's name	Year Built	Fleet list List	Fleet list Page	Illustration page(s)
ABERDONIAN (1)	1840	A11	56	
ABERDONIAN (2)	1909	B24	60	34, 37, 65
ABERDONIAN COAST	1947	B28	63	50
Ahmadi Coast	1948	B29	63	
BAN-RIGH	1870	B15	59	23
Beatriz	1910	B25	60	
BETSY	1826	A 4	55	
Bluestar	1906	B27	62	
Bolivar	1870	B15	59	
BON ACCORD	1824	A 3	55	
Caledonia	1876	B18	59	
CALEDONIAN COAST	1948	B29	63	51, 63
Chepo	1911	B26	62	
CITY OF ABERDEEN (1)	1835	B 3	57	57
CITY OF ABERDEEN (2)	1865	B14	59	
CITY OF ABERDEEN (3)	1873	B17	59	
CITY OF LONDON (1)	1844	B 6	58	14
CITY OF LONDON (2)	1871	B16	59	30, 38, 39
COMMODORE	1838	B10	58	
Dean Swift	1911	B26	62	
DUCHESS OF SUTHERLAND	1836	B 4	57	
DUKE OF SUTHERLAND	1847	B 7	58	
DUKE OF WELLINGTON	1829	B 2	57	
DUKE OF GORDON	1827	A 5	55	
DUKE OF ROTHESAY	1857	B11	58	
Durham Coast	1938	B30	63	
EARL OF ABERDEEN	1847	B 8	58	
El Brenon	1911	B26	62	
Elda	1942	B31	64	
Empire Atoll	1942	B31	64	
FLORENCE	1831	A 9	57	
G M La Vallette	1887	B21	60	
Gallus	1910	B25	60	
GAMBIA	1855	B12	58	
GAZELLE	1846	A14	56	
Gotha	1888	B23	60	
HADRIAN COAST	1942	B31	64	53
Hai Yang	1911	B26	62	
HARLAW (1)	1881	B20	60	
HARLAW (2)	1888	B23	60	
HARLAW (3)	1911	B26	62	35, 43
HEBRIDEAN COAST	1938	B30	63	65
HIBERNIAN COAST	1947	B28	63	
HOGARTH (1)	1876	B18	59	
HOGARTH (2)	1893	B22	60	23, 61
Hollina	1911	B26	62	
ICH DIEN	1877	B19	59	25, 30
Ionion	1887	B21	60	

Ship's name	Year Built	Fleet list		Illustration page(s)
		List	Page	
Kangaroo	1853	B12A	59	
KOOLGA	1910	B25	60	34, 41
Lairdswood	1906	B27	62	
Libertador	1870	B15	59	
Lochbroom	1871	B16	59	
LOCHNAGAR	1906	B27	62	35, 44, 47, 62
LONDON	1840	A12	56	
Makalla	1948	B29	63	
MANSFIELD	1802	A 2	55	
Margarita P	1938	B30	63	
Marroquin	1870	B15	59	
Min Yung	1910	B25	60	
Min Chih	1911	B26	62	
NIMROD	1817	A 1	55	
NORTH STAR	1837	B 5	58	
OITHONA	1887	B21	60	
PARAGON	1842	A10	56	
Parviz	1909	B24	60	
Port Said Coast	1947	B28	63	
QUEEN OF SCOTLAND	1827	B 1	57	8
Rena	1906	B27	62	
Rosalino Pilo	1835	B 3	57	
ROYAL VICTORIA	1835	B 9	58	
Salamis	1873	B17	59	
Sandhill	1938	B30	63	
Sinergasia	1938	B30	63	
Sonia	1938	B30	63	
STANLEY	1859	B13	59	
SUPERIOR	1814	A 7	56	
Swift	1911	B26	62	
Taishan Peak	1909	B24	60	
THETIS	1826	A 8	56	
Triumph	1911	B26	62	
TRUE BLUE	1827	A 6	55	
Ulster Chieftain	1938	B30	63	
VALERIAN COAST	1938	B30	63	50
Wicklow	1938	B30	63	
WILLIAM HOGARTH	1841	A13	56	
Woodcock	1906	B27	62	
Woodnut	1906	B27	62	
Yacout	1887	B21	60	

ACKNOWLEDGEMENTS

For help in the preparation of this history I am greatly indebted to many individuals, both past and present, and not least to the fact that some un-named person(s) within the Company ensured that most of the Minute Books, since its inception in 1836, were carefully stored away. They contained a wealth of information and detail that could never have been found anywhere else.

I am grateful for the help and assistance I received from the Special Collections and Archives Department of the University of Aberdeen for allowing me access to the Minute Books covering the period 1836 to 1925, and from the Manuscripts Section of the National Maritime Museum, Greenwich who are the keepers of those books covering the period 1940 onwards.

Illustrations and photographs have come from many sources and where this is known, then a suitable acknowledgement has been made. I am especially grateful to Mrs Catherine Walker, Assistant Curator of the Aberdeen Maritime Museum, for providing me with copies of the water colour paintings of some of the steamers by Mr D. McBain. Countless other individuals - too numerous to mention by name - have provided photographs and other material from their collections, and I appreciate their interest and generosity in allowing me to use their material.

Sincere thanks to the members of the Central Record team of The World Ship Society who provided me with additional information on the ships, to the staff of the Public Record Office, Kew, Surrey, the Reference Library, Guildhall, City of London, and the Scottish Record Office, Edinburgh, who produced the many files that I requested for inspection. On certain vital points I had need to approach Lloyd's Register of Shipping, London, and the Central Reference Library, Aberdeen and again I am most grateful for all the help and assistance that the staff of these organisations gave me.

Printed by The Amadeus Press Ltd, Huddersfield